BLACK HANDS, WHITE SAILS

BLACK

THE STORY OF

HANDS,

AFRICAN-AMERICAN

WHITE

WHALERS

SAILS

Patricia C. McKissack
& Fredrick L. McKissack

SCHOLASTIC PRESS / NEW YORK

Library of Congress Cataloging-in-Publication Data
McKissack, Pat, 1944–
Black hands, white sails: the story of African-American whalers /
by Patricia C. McKissack and Fredrick L. McKissack. p. cm
Includes bibliographical references (p.   ) and index.
Summary: A history of African-American whalers between 1730
and 1880, describing their contribution to the whaling industry
and their role in the abolition movement.
ISBN 0-590-48313-7 (hardcover)
1. Whaling — History — Juvenile literature.   2. Afro-American whalers —
Biography — Juvenile literature.   [1. Whaling — History.   2. Whalers.
3. Afro-Americans — Biography.]   I. McKissack, Fredrick.   II. Title.
SH381.5.M38 1999 639.2'8'0896073 — dc21 99-11439 CIP AC

10 9 8 7 6 5 4   0/0 1 2 3 4

Printed in the U.S.A. 23
First edition, October 1999
Book design by David Caplan

To John Fitzpatrick McKissack,
our grandson

CONTENTS

ACKNOWLEDGMENTS

Writing this book was an exciting journey of discovery. We have spent many enlightening hours at whaling museums, from Mystic, New Bedford, Nantucket, Boston, and Martha's Vineyard to San Francisco, Barbados, and Charleston. These were the places and people Herman Melville wrote so eloquently about in his great American novel *Moby Dick*, which we had read begrudgingly when we were in high school. Living in Nashville, miles from any ocean, we wondered what did the story about a captain driven by the obsession to kill a white whale have to do with the black experience in America? Plenty! After researching the nineteenth-century whaling industry, we discovered that the crew of the *Pequod* — Melville's fictional whaler — was very realistically represented. It was common practice that Yankee whale ships carried a racially mixed crew of blacks, Native Americans,

Africans, Cape Verdeans, West Indians, Pacific Islanders, and a wide assortment of Europeans.

Building on the research of historian Martha S. Putney, who researched material at the National Archives and at the Old Dartmouth Historical Society, we discovered that on whalers leaving New Bedford, "At least 3,189 identifiable blacks held positions on ships between 1803 to 1860. Ten percent of the crews leaving Newport, Rhode Island, were black. The same holds true for other whaling centers, including Nantucket and Salem." During the "golden age" of whaling (1800–60), African Americans comprised 25 percent of the whaling crews. And after the Civil War and well into the latter half of the nineteenth century, well over half the whaling crews were African Americans.

This time, when we read *Moby Dick,* we were drawn into the novel because we knew the history behind the story and we felt a part of it. We hope our readers will, after reading this book, also read one of America's best works of fiction with appreciation for its historical significance.

This book is about the African-American participation in the nineteenth-century whaling industry, but there is another thread that is woven throughout the book. The whalemen of Nantucket and New Bedford — both black and white — played an important role in the abolitionist movement and the Underground Railroad. This book is also about that movement.

We owe a debt of gratitude to many people who helped us achieve our goal. We thank all of those who directed our search through maritime documents, history, and photos for information. But most of all, we would like to thank our friends at the Kendall Whaling Museum in Sharon, Massachusetts, Mystic Seaport Museum in Connecticut, New Bedford Whaling Museum, Nantucket Whaling Museum, and the Martha's Vineyard Whaling Museum, whose collections of African-American whaling materials are invaluable to researchers. We relied upon the work of two excellent books about whaling, *A History of World Whaling* by Daniel Francis, and W. Jeffrey Bolster's *Black Jacks*. We thank the authors of these books for their impeccable research upon which we launched our own journey of discovery.

So come then, enjoy your own voyage —

> *Come, all ye jolly whalemen bold,*
> *And we will find them as of old.*
> *Listen till my tale is told.*
> *And listen till my tale is told.*

PATRICIA AND FREDRICK MCKISSACK
CHESTERFIELD, MISSOURI, 1999

"Now these three mates — Starbuck, Stubb, and Flask, were momentous men. They it was who by universal prescription commanded three of the Pequod's boats as headsmen. . . . And since in his famous fishery, each mate or headsman, like a Gothic Knight of old, is always accompanied by his boat-steerer or harpooneer. . . . First of all was Queequeg, whom Starbuck, the chief mate, had selected for his squire. . . . Next was Tashtego, an unmixed Indian from Gay Head, the most westerly promontory of Martha's Vineyard . . . which has long supplied the neighboring island of Nantucket with many of her most daring harpooneers. . . . Tashtego was Stubb the second mate's squire. . . . Third among the harpooneers was Daggoo. . . . In his youth Daggoo had voluntarily shipped on board of a whaler, lying in a lonely bay on his native coast [of Africa]. . . . There was a corporeal humility in looking up at him; and a white man standing before him seemed a white flag come to beg truce of a fortress. Curious to tell, this imperial negro, Ahasuerus Daggoo, was the Squire of little Flask, who looked like a chess-man beside him."

Moby Dick
HERMAN MELVILLE

INTRODUCTION

Whales are the largest mammals on earth. In the water they move with unparalleled grace and speed, unimpeded by any living creature — except humans. Long ago sailors feared these gentle, playful leviathans, certain that they were vicious sea monsters, capable of swallowing whole ships. Even when seamen no longer believed such myths, other incorrect information about whales still prevailed. For example, 150 years ago seamen thought whales were merely big fish. And it was through ignorance, and later greed, that men hunted whales almost to the point of extinction for their oil and baleen (whale bone).

But before it was too late, Americans led the international movement to "save the whale," and through the efforts of organizations such as Greenpeace, many countries have stopped hunting whales. Even though a few countries still do, the great herds are beginning to increase in numbers.

Two centuries ago, whaling was one of the most important industries in the world and the United States dominated the business. In 1847 there were 900 whale ships registered in the world. Of that number, 700 were American vessels registered from the major U.S. whaling ports: Nantucket, New Bedford, New London, Mystic, Sag Harbor, Providence, Cold Spring Harbor, and others.

These cities were also prosperous business centers where people were employed in supporting industries as shipbuilders, coopers, smiths, sail makers, caulkers, and provisioners. It was from the bustling cities that the whaling voyages began and ended. Today, whaleboats still depart from these same harbors, but they are now sightseeing vessels and the whale hunters are armed with harmless binoculars and cameras.

In 1978, three years after the environmental group Greenpeace began its campaign against commercial whaling, the sunken ruin of the *San Juan* was discovered in Red Bay off the shore of Labrador. The *San Juan* was a Basque whaling ship that had sunk during a hurricane in 1565, carrying a thousand casks of whale oil, valued in today's money at over six million dollars. The discovery of the *San Juan* shows us that a well-organized whaling industry was active in the New World not long after Columbus touched land at Hispaniola in the Caribbean.

A few years after the *San Juan* was located, divers found the bell of an English ship that had sunk in a hurricane off the coast of Florida, in 1701. Marine archaeologist David Moore joined a team of divers that began chipping away at centuries of encrustation and shells. At last they uncovered the year "1699." As they cleared away more, they found the words *Henrietta Marie*. It was the remains of a slave ship.

The significance of these two finds is that they indicated that whale ships and slave ships were a part of the growth and development of the American economy from the sixteenth through the nineteenth centuries. The slavers carried African captives who were the backbone of the New World agricultural economy. The whalers carried Africans, too, but as valued crew members. Where these two vessels intersect in history is when this story begins.

For thousands of years, people living near the oceans learned that whale oil burned longer and cleaner than other fuels. Archeological evidence suggests that the Inuit people of Alaska were hunting the whale when Ramses the Great was Pharaoh of Egypt. When Europeans arrived in the Americas they discovered that Native Americans were already master whale hunters. So, by combining what they knew from European whaling with the techniques they learned from the Indians, the colonists developed shore whaling into a profitable business at Long Island, Nantucket, and Cape Cod. Content at first to catch the occasional whale that drifted into shallow waters along the coast, the colonists soon learned how to build ships and hunt whales at sea.

A whale ship was a floating factory, specially designed with "tryworks" or special furnaces on board. This allowed crews to render the whale and store its oil in barrels. When the voyage ended, usually after two or three years at sea, the ship returned to various United States ports where the whales' oil was made into many marketable products, such as fuel for lamps, soap, smokeless candles, lubricant for machines, even bristles for brushes and brooms. The bones of the whales were ground up to make fertilizer for crops. Whale teeth were used to make decorative and useful items known as scrimshaw, carved by sailors during long voyages.

Life as a whaler was hazardous. The chance of a whaleman getting hurt, maimed, or killed at sea was twice that of a merchant seaman. The tours of duty on a whaler were long — the average voyage lasting from three to four years. The pay, called a "lay," was a miserably low percentage of the profit after all expenses were paid. Sometimes a seaman ended with little more than pennies a day for his hard work. Most times the treatment was so harsh and cruel, sailors abandoned the ship before the voyage ended. J. Ross Browne, a young whaleman, summarized it best when he wrote in 1840, "there is no class of men in the world, who are so unfairly dealt with, so oppressed, so degraded, as the seamen who man the vessels engaged in the American whale fishery."

The success of any voyage depended upon the crew. Aside from the captain, officers, cook, steward, and regular seamen, a whaling crew also included a coopersmith, a blacksmith, a carpenter, and several harpooners. Officers and craftsmen were usually experienced or from whaling families, and they were paid a higher lay. But since whaling was known for being difficult, demanding, and dangerous, the "ordinary crew" tended to be young and inexperienced. A large percentage were men of color — Native Americans, Cape Verdeans, West Indians, South Sea Islanders, and African Americans, many of whom were runaway slaves.

While the whaling industry was developing in the American colonies, slavery was taking hold as well. In 1619 Africans had been brought to the Virginia colony as indentured servants. By the end of the Revolutionary War, there were a million chattel slaves living in the United States.

Opposition to slavery was immediate and strong, beginning first among those slaves who resisted their condition. From sabotage to armed insurrections slaves used any opportunity to free themselves. Running away, however, was the most common form of rebellion. A surprising number of runaways were led to freedom via the Underground Railroad by both white and black sailors and captains. So many slaves were helped by seamen, one maritime historian noted that the Underground Railroad was virtually a ship. Once free, some fugitives wanted to help other captives escape, so they joined the ranks of those special sailors who were abolitionists. But it was very dangerous work that could lead to severe punishment and even death.

Unpredictable weather and work-related accidents were problems all sailors had to endure, but slavery and racism presented blacks with additional reasons for caution and concern. Free black seamen were sometimes kidnapped and enslaved while on leave in another slave country such as Cuba or Brazil. Some were even sold as slaves by their captains, or turned in to the authorities when they docked in a southern United States port.

Every whaling vessel was like a floating community at sea. Each had its own sense of "neighborhood," which reflected the moral standards of its captain, mates, and crew. A cruel, unfeeling captain usually mastered a cruel and indifferent crew. A strict but fair captain usually ran a tight ship where his men respected him even if they didn't always agree with his policies. A lazy captain's ship was predictably a disaster. The degree of racial tolerance and fairness extended to black crew members on board a ship was therefore established by the captain and his officers.

But black sailors had to find their own level of acceptance in the forecastle (crew quarters) and they did it in several different ways. A lot of whalemen earned the respect of their peers by being very good at their jobs, dependable, or strong. Others just looked tough enough to be left alone, while still others, young or small in stature, became clowns and entertainers in order to win approval.

One writer described a whale ship as "a blend of the best and the worst set of personalities ever assembled in one place." Blacks often found themselves among men who had been "educated in the first institutions in the country and had been in extensive and respectable business on shore." But they were also among men who were "of the most wicked and degraded families in the country . . . uninformed and disagreeable, and in many cases deplorably intemperate . . ." One crew member might defend a runaway to the death, but the next mate might turn him in to the authorities for reward money. And the cruel irony is that a black freeman might be the one to collect the bounty on a runaway's head.

Sometimes knowing the hardships and at other times blindly led by the fear of being captured, fugitive slaves still shipped out on whalers. The very circumstances that were considered unbearable to other men didn't seem to deter them. To a runaway, the sea gave him a chance to get far out of his master's reach. The possibilities of being captured and returned were lessened by distance. The pay, even though it was very low, was better than no pay at all. And even though the work was long and hard, the living quarters cramped and smelly, and the discipline harsh, to a slave it was better than being owned!

Free blacks also became sailors because it was one of the few jobs open to them. They especially turned to the whaling industry because of the Quakers' liberal hiring practices. A majority of whale shipowners and investors were New England Quakers, who were among the first groups to oppose slavery, even before it became an organized movement. Known for their piety, Quakers accepted any man who was fit and willing to sign on, regardless of race, color, or national origin — free or runaway. It was common knowledge that black hands were welcome to work among the white sails of Quaker ships.

This is not to suggest that all the Quakers' motives were purely altruistic, just as racism didn't magically disappear once a black sailor stepped on board a ship. Quakers were often criticized for practicing thrift in the extreme. Their harsher critics accused them of being penny-pinchers who made business decisions based entirely on profits and how to increase them. White sailors complained that they were victims of rigid Quaker management. Very often they were, but never to the degree that blacks were victimized.

The facts show that while the whaling industry was not as dehumanizing as slavery, many of the business practices condoned by shipowners, investors, and captains — many of them Quakers — were at times just as exploitative and brutal. There is no doubt the Quakers were business opportunists, but they cannot bear the full burden of responsibility for the unfair treatment of black whalemen. What made it worse for free blacks was the lack of alternative resources and the absence of support from the larger business community. There simply were no jobs available for them, so they were forced to find work wherever they could, under awful circumstances, and then try to make the best of it.

Consider this scenario. Two young men, the same age, same skills, same education, joined a whaling crew in 1847. They both were greenhorns hired to do the same work. They both completed the three-year voyage and returned to Sag Harbor. Both sailors had worked hard, eaten the same bad food, and missed their families equally as much. Neither one had made much money, but the black youth had earned even less. Parting, the white youth returned to his home where he took up farming, worked in the family business, or found a job in the city. But after a month of searching for a job, the black youth had no choice but to ship out again, because nobody would hire him.

Even though there were plenty of jobs in New England in the 1840s, free blacks had a hard time finding work. Why? It was standard practice that as long as there was a white who wanted a job, then an employer would not hire a black. And if the employer had to lay off a worker, all blacks were let go before the whites, regardless of seniority. Thus the saying, "Blacks are the last hired and first fired."

These discriminatory hiring practices became a boon for Quaker shipowners, who saw a chance to hire strong, willing men at the lowest possible price.

Though their motivation may have been questionable, Quakers still have to be credited with giving men the opportunity to work when other doors were closed to them. Some of these whalemen, who started at the bottom, managed to rise through the ranks and become officers and even shipowners. So when there were crew calls, men of color were in no short supply.

In time, some black whalemen became prominent, well-respected members of their community, inventors, businessmen, and abolitionists. They were well-traveled, knowledgeable men who were often literate and self-confident. They had fought a creature the size of a building, so they were not likely to think of themselves as inferior to any man. And after seeing their accomplishments and earning respect for their skills, some of their white counterparts weren't so willing to think of black men as subhuman creatures designed by a lesser god. White whalemen came to realize that blacks, when given the opportunity, could match their skills on land and sea. Therefore the abolitionists found great recruits among young, white seamen. And it is no wonder that the whaling communities of Nantucket and New Bedford were strongholds of the nineteenth-century antislavery movement.

All whalers — men and women, blacks and whites — set themselves apart from other seafaring people; they had their own songs and stories, and their own ideas about fairness. The African-American presence in the whaling industry and their involvement in the struggle for freedom and justice in America are but footnotes in most maritime histories. Their story is like a small but significant puzzle piece that, when lost, leaves a hole in the big picture. But when the information in this book is placed within the proper historical context, the same as a missing puzzle piece, the American story becomes more complete and clearer.

CHAPTER ONE

SHORE WHALING

LIQUID GOLD

When the Pilgrims arrived in North America in 1620, they joyfully recorded that there were "hordes of whales in the coastal waters," and their new home was "a place of profitable fishing."

The Indians were already experienced whalers and master harpooners whose accuracy was sure. Captain George Weymouth, an English explorer, described how Indians hunted a whale off the coast of Maine circa 1620. "They surround the whale with a multitude of their [small] Boats," he wrote, "and strike him with a Bone made in fashion of a harping iron [harpoon] fastened to a rope. . . ." Then after stabbing and jabbing the whale with lances, they waited for it to die from the loss of blood. Hauling the animal back to shore, they cut it into pieces and distributed it among their community.

The colonists also noted that the killing of a whale was accompanied by a great deal of ceremony and celebration in the Indian villages. The whale was honored and every part of it was used for some good purpose, much the way the Plains Indians honored the buffalo in story and song and used all its parts. There is no evidence that the Indians ever endeavored to make whaling a business venture. But the colonists did right away. And black men were a part of the process from the beginning — first as slave laborers, then as freemen.

Whale oil was a sought-after commodity; to get it colonists had to wait either for a whale to wash up on shore and be quickly processed before it spoiled, or they had to pay a large price for processed oil to be shipped from England. Neither was practical, so Massachusetts colonists began whale hunting, using the same methods as the Indians. In time, they improved their harpoons and the boats. Then in the 1640s, settlers moved from Massachusetts to Long Island, and there the American whaling business began.

Through careful observation and records, Long

Islanders learned that November to June was the ideal whaling time, as this old saying suggests:

June, too soon.
July, stand by.
August, look out you must.
September, remember.
October, all over.

During the whaling season, Long Islanders, including slaves, free blacks, and Indians, constructed towers that overlooked the sea. They stationed watchers in these towers, which resembled a ship's tall mast. Up there, men took shifts to look for passing whales. When one was spied, the lookout called, "Whale off," and ran up a flag. It was usually a right whale, called so because it was large, slow-moving, and could yield up to one hundred barrels of oil. In all ways it was the "right whale" to catch.

Once the flag was raised, six appointed men would get into a boat and sail out to the whale and kill it. They were usually Indians, employed for the purpose of harpooning. In 1672 the governor of New York passed a law that tried to regulate the price Indians were paid for their services. But by 1709, the Indian had become so important to the shore whaling industry, Parliament enacted a law stating:

"for the encouragement of Whaling, any Indians bound to go to sea whale fishing between November 1 and April 15 following, should not be arrested or kept out of employment under any pretense of a contract or debt . . ."

This act was enforced through 1726 and perhaps even longer. A person could also be fined for selling alcohol to an Indian during whaling season.

Once the whale had been killed, it was brought back to shore where it was "tried out." First the bone was removed, then the blubber was boiled inside a big iron kettle called a "try-pot." The smell was awful, but the product was pure oil, as valuable as gold. In some places whale oil was even used as money. Records show that an East Hampton schoolmaster was partially paid with whale oil. It was not uncommon for a daughter to be given whale oil as a wedding gift from her father or father-in-law.

When the whale was rendered, a portion was divided among the hunters and the townspeople. A few good catches meant that people had clean-burning fuel for lamps and lubricant for machinery. Whalebone was used for hoopskirts, corsets, and umbrella frames.

All oil that was left over was sold, and the community shared in whatever profits were made. Along with farming, whaling offered economic independence and stability to these early whaling communities. That's why when a whale was sighted, schools and businesses closed, and everybody took part in some way. The only industry more profitable for investors was slavery.

BLACK GOLD

Just as fortunes were being made selling whale oil, they were also being made trafficking slaves, and there was no end to the number of investors willing to sponsor at least one leg in the slave trade.

Three continents formed what was known as slavery's "Triangle Trade." The first part of the voyage began when European ships from Portugal, Spain, England, the Netherlands, France, Denmark, and Sweden set out for the west coast of Africa. These ships carried a variety of goods that were traded with Arabs and Africans in exchange for African captives — black gold.

The second part of the triangle was the infamous transatlantic crossing known as the "Middle Passage."

Placed on a ship, many for the first time, the African captives endured an unspeakable nightmare. Arriving in an American port some months later, the captives who survived were sold like cattle and put to work.

The base of the triangle was the return trip to Europe. Sugar, coffee, tobacco, and rice grown in the colonies by slave labor were loaded on ships and taken to European ports and sold. Then the cycle began again and continued as long as there were profits to be made.

The first African captives in the North American colonies were brought to Jamestown, Virginia, in August of 1619. A total of twenty men and women were accorded the status of "indentured servants," which meant they would work for a period of seven years and then be freed. Massachusetts was the first colony to legalize chattel, or slavery for life, in 1641. Connecticut followed in 1650, and New York and New Jersey in 1664. North Carolina did not legalize slavery until 1715.

Slave hands helped in the building of American farms, commerce, and industry since the earliest days of colonization. The whaling business was no exception. Slave labor was used in shore whaling on Long Island, in Massachusetts, and wherever it was practiced. But almost immediately there was conflict over the issue of owning a human being the way one would own a dog or a horse.

The first people to oppose slavery were blacks themselves, who petitioned legally for their freedom in places such as New York and Virginia. When basic rights were denied even freed blacks, then more desperate means were used to gain their freedom. With the help of free blacks and a few whites, slaves used sabotage, ran away, or committed other rebellious acts. In time others joined in the struggle for freedom and justice. At a time when the whale oil business was on the rise, there was also a slowly developing conflict over slavery. At the core of this economic and social growth were the Nantucket Quakers.

NANTUCKET — A FAR-OFF PLACE

According to the Indians, a giant named Maushop lived on Cape Cod. He loved to sleep under an open sky along the beach. But sand filled his moccasins. When he awoke one morning with his shoes filled with sand, he kicked them off and one became *Noepe* (Martha's Vineyard) and the other became *Natokete* or Nantucket, which means a "far-off place."

The myth contains elements of truth, for Nantucket is a small island located off Cape Cod, Massachusetts. It is no more than fourteen miles long from end to end, largely a low, sandy place, covered with stiff grasses and dotted with ponds, swamps, and stunted vegetation.

During an exploration of the area in 1602, Captain Bartholomew Gosnold claimed Cape Cod and the islands of Nantucket and Martha's Vineyard as British possessions. By 1641 the islands were owned by two English lords, who sold them to Thomas Mayhew, a rich New England merchant. As a Puritan, Mayhew wanted to Christianize the Indians who lived there. He began with the Gay Head Indians of Martha's Vineyard, and soon the island had a settlement.

Tristram Coffin, Thomas Macy, and seven other men purchased Nantucket from Mayhew for thirty pounds sterling — a little over fifty dollars. Two beaver hats, status symbols of the day, were also part of the bargain: "one for myself and one for my wife," Mayhew put in the contract.

The first colonial settlers landed on Nantucket in the fall of 1659. Among the founding members were names that became synonymous with whaling and the abolitionist movement in Massachusetts — people such as John Swain and Christopher Hussey.

In search of a place where they could practice their religion freely, a Massachusetts Quaker missionary paid a visit to Nantucket in 1702. At a gathering at the home of a prominent family, the Society of Friends made its first island convert. The Friends set roots that grew well in Nantucket's soil. But who were the Quakers and what did they believe?

Members of the Society of Friends were no strangers to persecution. Since their beginning in 1647, they were punished for their beliefs. The Society was founded by an Englishman, George Fox (1624–91), who taught that a person should live by a strict code of conduct in which honesty, thrift, and hard work were essential. Quakers shunned all worldly activities — fighting, gambling, music, drama, art, dancing, and cardplaying. Fox further taught that God's will would be made known to men and women without priests or ministers and without rituals and sacraments. These ideas were considered extreme and the Friends were punished severely. It is said that Fox admonished an English judge, saying, "You should quake at the word of the Lord." And since many Friends did tremble during their meetings, they became known as Quakers.

Unfortunately, Puritans who came to the New World in search of religious freedom were not very tolerant of other religions, especially Quakers. At least three Quakers were hanged in Massachusetts between 1659 and 1661 because of their beliefs.

William Penn, a convert to Quakerism, founded Pennsylvania in 1681. There the Friends could practice their faith peacefully. Passage of the Toleration Act of 1689 by the English Parliament helped alleviate religious persecution in the colonies, though it never really ended, because the act only covered some religions.

The Quakers' beliefs were as simple as their clothing and houses. At a Quaker meeting, no minister presided. Men sat on one side of the meetinghouse and women sat on the other, but women were considered equal to men. There were no hymns sung, no rituals followed. When the Spirit moved a member, he or she spoke before the entire congregation.

Quakers opposed taxes, capital punishment, and slavery. They were the first group in the New World to take a stand against slavery, and they defined their position in a formal protest, issued during a monthly meeting on February 18, 1688. They declared that slavery and the slave trade were evil. It was the beginning of a long and bitter battle between the two opposing sides of slavery, but the Quaker position never wavered until slavery ended. Quakers opened schools for blacks in Philadelphia and, in 1758, Philadelphia Quakers voted to exclude anyone who bought or sold slaves from participating in the meetings and affairs of the church. Other Quaker groups followed their lead.

Quakers took to whaling with as much passion as they did social issues. In 1672 a delegation of

Nantucket businessmen asked James Lopar of Long Island to come and teach them what he knew about shore whaling. For reasons that remain unknown he did not stay long on the island. In 1690 Nantucketers again tried to find a tutor and this time they were successful. Ichabod Paddock of Cape Cod accepted the offer and moved to Nantucket.

The principal shore whaling industry remained on Long Island at Sag Harbor but, by 1700, Nantucket had become the center of both the whaling and the antislavery movements.

CHAPTER TWO

GONE A-WHALING

OUT TO SEA

In 1712 Captain Christopher Hussey and his crew left Nantucket harbor on a routine whale hunt. But it turned out not to be so ordinary. Their vessel was a single-sail ship called a sloop that had been outfitted as a whaler. A few hours out, they encountered a storm that swept them away from the shoreline and far out into the open sea.

Out there the raging storm tossed the sloop about like a cork. But suddenly the lookout spotted a school of whales passing by. "Whale off," he called.

In a daring move, Captain Hussey decided to take on a healthy whale in the open water in the middle of a storm. His men were with him, driven no doubt by the profits they would share, so when Hussey ordered them to lower the smaller boat, they obeyed. For the first time in New England whaling, men fought a whale in its own territory — the open seas. With the storm still raging, they pursued it and made their catch. Then they used the dead whale's huge body as a protective shield until the storm passed over. Towing it back to shore, they were delighted that it was a sperm whale.

News spread quickly that a sperm whale had been taken in waters farther out than ever before. And contrary to what had been believed, the sperm whale was discovered to move in herds. So investors got busy and outfitted ships that could go hunt whales out to sea.

Before Captain Hussey's success, a dead whale had to be brought back to shore where it was tried out. The farther ships sailed from shore, the more difficult it was to get the whale back before the sharks attacked it or it spoiled. The answer was to redesign whale ships and equip them with the tryworks on board. Now the whale could be caught at sea, rendered there, and the oil stored in barrels. With ships like these, crews could travel farther and stay out longer.

The improved Nantucket whale ships carried smaller boats that were lowered into the water when a whale was spotted. Then, rowing close to their target, the harpooner struck with lethal accuracy. There was very little margin for error, because the whale was attached to the boat by a rope tied to the harpoon. Wherever the whale went so did the boat.

If the whale decided to run, then the crew was in for a rough ride known as a Nantucket Sleigh Ride in which the whale could haul them for miles at twice or three times its normal speed. If the whale sounded, it would suddenly plunge deep into the water, diving fast and straight down. If the ropes weren't cut immediately, the small boat would be dragged under. Sometimes a dying whale might breach, rising up out of the water like an island, and overturn and crush everything in the wake of its powerful tail. A few whales, though not many, turned on their attackers and sank ships. If the crew survived all these possibilities and managed to hold on, the sperm whale eventually died and was tried out.

Whaling was not for the weak. The men who hunted whales were different from most sailors. So they wouldn't be confused with other men, seamen set themselves apart in several ways. They pulled their hair back in tightly worked queues. They wore earrings and decorated their bodies with tattoos. Each was as tough as leather and as salty as a sea breeze. When someone wanted to describe a man who was bold, strong, and wildly daring, they referred to him as a "Nantucket Whaleman."

NANTUCKET'S BLACK WHALEMEN

It was widely known that the seamen who manned Nantucket vessels were multinational and multiracial. At first, however, the crews were members of Nantucket's whaling families. Indians and blacks also made up the crew.

The first black whalemen of Nantucket were slaves brought there in 1716, just four years after Captain Hussey's historic whale hunt. As the Quaker population grew in size and authority, their opposition to slavery became more forceful. Nantucketers began freeing their slaves voluntarily. Some of these freed people were the founders of Nantucket's proud black whaling families.

Soon mainlanders were attracted by the island's strong economic potential and they came to the island, too. Free blacks were drawn there for employment opportunities. But the fugitive slaves knew that among the Quakers they could enjoy relative safety and freedom.

Even though Quakers might have been socially liberal, their influence stopped at land's end. Some of the officers and mates who manned their ships were indifferent or didn't share their employer's views about race. Once out at sea, men of color were often at the mercy of bigoted captains, prejudiced mates, and racist crew members.

J. Ross Browne, a white southerner who served on a Yankee whaler, wrote that it was "insufferable" to live with a black sailor who thought himself "equal to any white man onboard." But Browne and others like him soon learned that when hurricane winds were blowing or their boat was attached to the end of a raging bull sperm whale, it didn't matter what color the hands were that handled the sails or pulled the oars. The rules were clear. All men had to work together if they were to survive. This reality is what earned blacks respect, or at least they were tolerated, even though they were not always accepted.

Quakers were not blameless in the exploitation of blacks, either. All "ordinary" whalemen — those without rank or skill — were paid miserably low wages, a kind of profit-sharing arrangement similar to late nineteenth- and early twentieth-century sharecropping. Their pay was called a "lay," and represented a percentage of the net value of the cargo. Owners took up to 50 percent of the profit. Captains were usually paid a lay of 1/8th to 1/10th. A "greenie," a sailor on his first voyage, might get as little as 1/250th.

All money was disbursed at the end of the voyage when the size of the cargo was tallied and the sailor's "expenses" were deducted. Sailors were advanced money and the cost of their clothing, tobacco, equipment, and other personal items, which they purchased from the ship's store, were taken out of their lay. Sometimes sailors returned home owing money to the owners.

Various studies of whaling logs and other records show that the lays of blacks were lower than whites who had the same qualifications. And according to one report, blacks were deliberately mistreated toward the end of the voyage in an effort to make them leave the ship and forfeit their lay.

Black whalemen knew they were being discriminated against but they were powerless to change anything. They had to either accept the arrangement or find work somewhere else. But where else could they find work? One way was to build businesses for themselves and capitalize their own whaling ventures. And that's what they did.

Blacks formed a community named New Guinea, located south of Nantucket City. There, a mixed population of Indians and blacks — that grew to over 300 men, women, and children — built houses, businesses, meetinghouses, and attended school and churches. Most of the permanent residents were connected to the whaling industry, and jobs created the financial stability necessary for successful growth.

PRINCE BOSTON

Several years before the American Revolution, William Swain, a Nantucket seaman who owned a whaler, signed papers dated July 31, 1760, freeing a slave, Boston, his wife Maria, and their youngest son Peter. They were freed, according to Swain, "in Consideration of the Many good & faithful Services . . . Done me."

Boston and Maria's other six children were to remain slaves until they reached age twenty-eight. This was a common form of gradual emancipation that was used to end slavery in several northern colonies. In Nantucket documents and records, the children are listed with their father's first name as their last name.

Prince Boston, for example, was born March 15, 1750. He was one of the sons who was not freed and remained Swain's slave. As was the custom with some slaveholders, Prince was a "hire out" on the Nantucket whaler *Friendship*, and his lay was to be given to his master. The ship was owned by William Rotch, who was opposed to slavery, as was the captain of the *Friendship*, Elisha Folger.

When the vessel returned, Rotch ordered Captain Folger to pay Prince Boston directly. Swain was angry and took the case to court, but the judge upheld Rotch. Swain then appealed in the Massachusetts Supreme Court. But he dropped the case when he realized he had very little public support, and besides, Rotch was going to hire a fiery young lawyer by the name of John Adams to handle the case. As a direct result of this action, slavery was abolished on the island of Nantucket, even though it wasn't until 1783 that slavery was finally abolished throughout the Commonwealth of Massachusetts.

Boston and Maria became the heads of a large and well-respected family of Nantucket seamen. They purchased property and became businesspeople. Besides Prince, Boston and Maria's son Tobias was also a whaler. Essex earned a living as a shoemaker and Seneca became a fine weaver. Seneca married Thankful, a Native American, and their youngest son became a whaling captain.

In the meantime the thirteen American colonies fought a war to free themselves from England. Two incidents that led up to the war, which began in 1776, were the Boston Massacre and the Boston Tea Party, both of which whalers and whalemen took part in.

THE REVOLUTIONARY WAR AND WHALING

Crispus Attucks, a mulatto, was a veteran seaman and whaler. He was one of five people killed in the so-called Boston Massacre, on March 5, 1770.

Attucks ran away from his master and in 1750 went to sea on a whale ship. While on leave, Attucks attended meetings and frequented places where activists such as Samuel Adams were giving stirring speeches about freedom and justice. Attucks and Samuel Adams became acquainted.

It was close to spring, but it was still winter in Boston. Snow covered the ground outside the tavern where Attucks was socializing with friends. Attucks was described as a likable man even though his size was imposing. He stood well over 6 feet 4 inches tall. And no doubt, like most black tars of his day, he had a certain confidence that made him appear arrogant to many whites.

When the gathering broke up, there was a confrontation between a group of colonists. Told to move on by the British soldiers on guard, Attucks and the crowd refused to obey. Heated words were exchanged.

Then Attucks and the others threw snowballs. In the confusion, shots were fired into the crowd. Five people were killed and six others were wounded. Counted among the dead was Attucks.

Sam Adams seized the opportunity to make Attucks a martyr for the cause of liberty. It was he who used the word "massacre," although the facts did not fit the term. On March 5, and every year thereafter, Adams published a pamphlet reminding colonists of the incident. To African Americans, Crispus Attucks became a hero, honored to this day as "one of the first Americans to die for his nation's liberty."

Two whaling ships, the *Dartmouth* of New Bedford and the *Beaver* of Nantucket, were involved in another dramatic historical incident leading up to the Revolutionary War. In 1773 the ships had delivered a load of whale oil to London. Then they were hired by the East India Company to deliver a load of tea to Boston.

Back home in the colonies, revolutionary forces were reacting to the passage of the Tea Act. The East India Company, one of the giant trading businesses in the world, had a huge supply of tea. The company's friends in Parliament pushed through the Tea Act, which allowed the company to sell its surplus tea at a price that undercut colonial merchants and established a monopoly in the tea trade. Once again, Boston radicals took the lead in protesting the act.

The two whaling ships, filled with tea, arrived and docked in Boston Harbor next to the English ship *Eleanor*. On the night of December 16, 1773, a group of fifty rebels, disguised as Indians, boarded the ships and dumped 342 chests of tea into the water. Known as the "Boston Tea Party," the protest became one of the small fires that eventually ignited the flames of war.

The Revolutionary War began in 1776. And for the most part, the American whaling industry was devastated. The British fleet captured whalers and looted homes on the mainland as well as Nantucket and Martha's Vineyard. By the time the war ended in 1781, over 1,200 American seamen had been captured or killed, and 134 ships were seized — among them a large number of Yankee whale ships.

But the prospect of freedom bolstered the rebels' courage and leaders of the fledgling nation immediately began the process of defining the future of their country. Naturally, the question of slavery was an issue that had to be dealt with in writing the United States Constitution. Many New Englanders wanted to abolish slavery. To their disappointment, however, on September 17, 1787, the United States Constitution was approved in Philadelphia with three clauses that protected slavery. It was a devastating blow to African Americans, who felt betrayed. They had fought and died in support of the revolution, believing that the promises in the Declaration of Independence included them. They were angered by the hypocrisy of the "peculiar institution" where democracy tried to coexist with slavery. It was wrong and they started organizations to resist it. Not surprisingly, Quakers became the allies of blacks in this struggle. Pro-slavery advocates were becoming more and more concerned about the number of whites, some of them elected officials, who were beginning to attack slavery as well.

The most formidable movement among the abolitionists was the escape route known as the Underground Railroad. It was neither underground nor a railroad, but rather a metaphor for a secret group of nameless, faceless people (conductors) who organized routes (a railroad) by which runaway slaves made their way from one safe house (station) to another until they reached freedom in the North. Very often the way to freedom was not by land, but by sea. Countless slaves made it to freedom with the help of a "black Jack," a black seaman, or a Nantucket whaleman.

Between the end of the Revolutionary War and the War of 1812, Britain continued to harass Americans.

One particularly aggravating form of British bullying was the impressment of American sailors. British battleships stopped American vessels at sea and boarded them, under the pretense that they were looking for English deserters. If a seaman didn't have identification or couldn't prove that he was an American citizen, the British could force him into service. To protect white sailors from impressment, the new United States government began issuing them passports. These documents were called "sailor's protection certificates."

SAILOR'S PROTECTION CERTIFICATES

Though not designed to protect black seamen, the certificates benefited them more than ever imagined. First, anybody could receive a sailor's protection certificate at any port where there was a United States collector of customs. All that was required was a birth certificate or some other proof of citizenship. In addition, an African American had to show his emancipation documents to verify that he was free.

Since no photographs were available at that time for identification purposes, a description was included on the certificate, so an official could be sure it belonged to the person carrying it. Often a seaman used his free papers and sailor's protection documents to help runaways get their own forged documents, or let them borrow them to escape. If caught, a sailor could be fined and jailed, so getting involved was very dangerous. Some sailors exploited the situation and made a profit by selling forged certificates to runaways. And one of the first places a runaway headed was Nantucket.

Except for a downturn during the War of 1812, whaling recovered and within a decade was one of the most profitable businesses in the United States. The time period between 1815 and 1865 is called the Golden Age of Whaling. And in spite of all the devastation, Nantucket rebounded and became the leading port in the industry.

CHAPTER THREE

BLACK WHALEMEN OF NANTUCKET

BLACK WHALING CAPTAINS

It wasn't likely that a man who had hunted a creature 400 times his size would not have a sense of self-pride. He usually held his head a little higher and pulled his shoulders back a little farther. There is a portrait of a sea captain with strong features and inquisitive eyes that hangs in the Whaling Museum of Nantucket. The sign next to the picture identifies the man as Captain Absalom Boston (1785–1855), a whaling master.

Boston was from a long tradition of seafaring men from the all-black Nantucket community of New Guinea. He was the nephew of Prince Boston, who had helped end slavery on the island. Young Absalom began his career as a mariner in 1800 when he shipped out as an ordinary seaman. In the census records, he was listed as "black man mariner."

While still in his twenties, he retired after making several voyages. By age thirty-five he had become a barber and owner of a public inn in New Guinea.

Boston made at least one last whaling voyage in 1822 as the captain of his own ship, leaving Nantucket on the whaling schooner *Industry*. Referred to as "noble black tars" by fellow Nantucketers, the all-black crew of the *Industry* left for Mexico the same year that another former seaman, Denmark Vesey, planned a slave rebellion in Charleston, South Carolina. Boston's trip was successful. Unfortunately, Vesey was betrayed and hanged.

Most whale ships stayed out as long as three years or more, but the *Industry* returned in six months with seventy barrels of oil. The reason for the quick return was not given, but whatever the reason, the ship was sold at auction, the lays paid, and the investors compensated. With all accounts settled, the voyage was considered successful.

Captain Boston was a leader on land as well as at sea. He married twice and had eight children, most of whom died at early ages. But he built an inn, a dance hall, and even helped establish a black school on Nantucket.

When gold was discovered in California in 1849, many Nantucketers left the island in search of their fortunes out West. But the Bostons remained along with many of the older black families, such as the Pompeys, Godfreys, Harrises, and others.

Absalom Boston died on June 6, 1855, on Nantucket where he had lived all his life, and he was buried in the Old South, or the black, cemetery. He left his heirs one thousand dollars, "a home, a store, two other houses, a garden lot on York Street, and a mowing lot on Pleasant Street." This was a sizable estate by the standards of that day.

Interestingly enough, the last Boston referenced in Nantucket history was Benajah C. Boston, the great-grandson of Boston and Maria, and a second cousin of Absalom. In 1864 he appeared on a roster of young men of eligible age to serve in the state militia. Next to Benajah's name is the phrase "at sea."

Absalom Boston was not the first or the last black man to captain a ship. On August 27, 1823, a year after the *Industry*'s voyage, the whaler *John Adams* arrived at Nantucket, skippered by Peter Green, a black crew member who was the second mate. Captain Marrick and the first mate had been lost while chasing a whale, so Green had taken charge and sailed the ship back to safe harbor.

Captain Bunker of the *Paragon* had in 1825 noted in his logbook that he had come across the *Hunter* adrift in the mid-Atlantic. She had lost her captain and first mate and no other crew member could navigate. Captain Bunker called on a black member of his crew whom he knew could navigate, and assigned him to the *Hunter*.

And on September 7, 1830, the whaling ship *Loper* returned to Nantucket with 2,280 barrels of oil. The owners, including the captain, Obed Starbuck, gave a dinner in honor of the crew, who were almost entirely black, which was followed by a parade. At that time, parades were used to advertise an event, to garner support for an issue, or to celebrate. On this occasion it was a parade of celebration.

Blacks on Nantucket welcomed the open display of gratitude and acceptance, because the issue of slavery that had divided the nation into two political camps was also affecting Nantucket. Northern whites opposed slavery in varying degrees but it was never a unified or unanimous movement. Some Northerners favored a gradual emancipation plan that had been used in New Jersey and New York. Theodore Weld of Ohio wanted slaves to be freed after they were educated, and to that end, he formed the Liberty Party in 1840. Other abolitionists pushed hard for an immediate end to all slavery, and there were those who chose to use force.

William Lloyd Garrison, a Bostonian, was the leader of the most militant group of antislavery sympathizers. As publisher of *The Liberator*, an antislavery journal first issued on January 1, 1831, and as founder of the American Anti-Slavery Society in 1833, Garrison wrote, "I am earnest — I will not equivocate — I will not excuse — I will not retreat an inch — AND I WILL BE HEARD."

Everyone knew where Garrison stood with regard to slavery. He was totally committed. But some of his contemporaries were not as sure. Attitudes about African Americans — both free and black — were very often complicated, contradictory, and hard to understand. For example, one white family was perfectly willing to risk their lives to help a runaway slave escape, but they were unwilling to allow their children to attend school with a free black child. Absalom Boston had tried to enroll his daughter, Phebe Ann, in the all-white Nantucket high school and she was refused.

Even Quakers, who were among the first to oppose slavery, felt that whites, blacks, and Indians were better off separated from each other, justifying their position by citing God's command in Genesis — "each to its own kind." The Quakers did not go so far as to restrict blacks from joining the Friends the way some denominations did. And one of their black members agreed that separation was the only way to insure peace and equality between the races. Captain Paul Cuffe, an African-American shipbuilder, captain, businessman, and social activist, believed that there wasn't a way for free blacks to get fair treatment in the United States, so he devoted his life to a Back-to-Africa movement.

CAPTAIN PAUL CUFFE (1759–1817)

Paul Cuffe, was born on the small island of Cuttyhunk, located off the coast of Westport, Massachusetts. In 1603 Captain Bartholomew Gosnold, an English explorer, noted that Cuttyhunk was a good "place of rendezvous." Using the island as a base, he explored the coastline of Massachusetts and traded with the Wampanoag Indians, who called the island *Poochutohhunkunooh*, from which Cuttyhunk is a shortened version.

John Slocum purchased Paul Cuffe's father, an African who was about twenty-eight years old, in 1742. Slocum renamed him Cuffe Slocum. Cuffe was an industrious man, for within two years he had done extra work and earned enough money to purchase his freedom. He then married Ruth Moses, a Wampanoag woman. Together they had ten children — four sons and six daughters. Paul Cuffe was born January 17, 1759. By then his family had dropped Slocum as their surname and used their father's first name instead.

When Daddy Cuffe died, he left the family's 116-acre farm to his sons Paul, who was age fourteen, and John. It was hard to scratch a living out of the rocky and unproductive soil of Cuttyhunk. So, like thousands of youngsters had before him, Paul went to sea the year he turned sixteen.

During his third voyage the Revolutionary War had started, and his ship was captured by the British. He was held prisoner of war for three months in New York. Fortunately, he wasn't sold into slavery. After his release in 1779, Paul rejoined his family, who had by then moved to Westport.

Feeling responsible for his family, Paul looked for ways to support them. Though only twenty, he and another brother, David, built an open boat and used it to trade with retailers in Connecticut and Nantucket. It proved to be a profitable business selling dried meat and other provisions. Paul learned thrift from his Quaker neighbors and saved a portion of every dollar he earned.

Finally, he had saved up enough to invest in a ship. It was similar to buying stock in a company today. When that money earned him a profit, he reinvested it in another ship. By the time he was twenty-five, in 1784, Paul Cuffe had earned enough to buy and master his own vessel.

Married since 1783 to Alice Pequit, a Wampanoag Indian like his mother, Captain Cuffe began raising their six daughters and two sons. He spent as much time as he could at the family compound in Westport, where he had built his farmhouse near the shore. There he had a wonderful view of his wharf and storehouse.

It was about this time that the industrious young man became friends with William Rotch, Jr. In 1765, Rotch, a wealthy Nantucket Quaker, who had played a major role in the freeing of Prince Boston, moved his shipbuilding and whaling company to New Bedford on the mainland. Joseph Russell joined him, and together they gave New Bedford its start as a whaling port.

Rotch liked Cuffe's zeal and good business sense. They became personal friends and business associates. Rotch also introduced Captain Cuffe to John James and Samuel Fisher, who were Philadelphia Quakers. They also took an interest in him.

His friends taught him that by applying sound business practices, he would gain the confidence of investors. Captain Cuffe must have taken the advice to heart, because he offered shares in his shipping ventures and raised the capital to expand his business.

According to Cuffe's biographer, George Salvador, "By 1800, Captain Cuffe had extended his area of trade from cod-fishing to shipping cargo to Boston, Philadelphia, Wilmington, Norfolk, Savannah, and the West Indies."

While slaves were still the cargo of American ships going and coming from West Africa, whale ships also had reason to look toward Africa. The Atlantic had been "fished out" by the mid-1700s. But whales were sighted off the coast of West Africa. Cuffe happened to be at the right time and place to capitalize on these new hunting grounds. He made several prosperous whaling voyages to Africa, where he visited many African nations.

Most of Captain Cuffe's ships were commanded by his relatives and manned by all-black crews. By 1806 Cuffe owned three brigs, one schooner, and several smaller vessels. And he'd expanded his trade to Europe and Africa. He converted most of his profits into real estate and investment property, but an idea was developing slowly in his mind.

Cuffe's friends and associates had helped him move in circles that were closed to most blacks of his day. But his heart was troubled. It bothered Cuffe that even with his impeccable reputation, white seamen were reluctant to sign on under him, because he was a black man. He struggled with the knowledge that black craftsmen paid more for their supplies than whites, and that meant their finished goods had to cost more. It was even more troubling that Captain Cuffe was affluent, well liked, and successful, yet as a Massachusetts citizen he could not serve on a jury, and his children could not attend integrated schools. Even interracial marriages were not legal — except among blacks and Indians. Although Cuffe had enough money to buy any of the local inns and restaurants, he and his fellow free blacks were forced to eat in a section with a curtain drawn around it or in the kitchen with the servants. Over and over, Captain Cuffe heard the horror stories of how free blacks were chased out of opera houses and denied the right to buy a home for their families outside their all-black neighborhoods.

Cuffe, who was a pious man, was even more concerned about the churches. Blacks were allowed to attend, but they were forced to sit in segregated corners. Such an incident had led Richard Allen in 1787 to leave St. George's Church in Philadelphia and start the African Methodist Episcopal Church. In an unusual move in 1808, Captain Cuffe became a Quaker. It was possible, though not common, for blacks to join the Friends. When they did they were fully accepted as members. Captain Cuffe was well respected, but it didn't hurt to have powerful friends such as Rotch supporting his membership.

Throughout New England, blacks were organizing to protest this overt discrimination and Paul Cuffe became a leader. Not one to complain, he set about finding a solution to the problems his people faced, using whatever resources were available to him.

Captain Cuffe tried in as many ways as he knew how to improve the condition of free black people in the United States, but conditions didn't get any better. Sadly, he came to the conclusion that the only way for blacks to be truly free was to return to Africa and set up a colony. England and France had already begun the recolonization of their freed blacks, and Cuffe was in communication with the leaders of the West African colony of Sierra Leone.

In 1816 Captain Cuffe transported thirty-eight free blacks to Sierra Leone. This much-publicized voyage raised interest among whites, but it also caused outrage within some black communities.

It was through Paul Cuffe's efforts that the American Colonization Society was formed on December 18, 1817. The society purchased a strip of land off the west coast of Africa and named it Liberia, from a Latin word meaning "free."

But other African Americans disagreed with Captain Cuffe and the Back-to-Africa plan. In January 1817, there was a meeting at the newly formed Bethel African Methodist Episcopal Church in Philadelphia "to take into consideration the propriety of remonstrating against the contemplated measure, that is to exile us from the land of our nativity."

The meeting was chaired by James Forten, a black entrepreneur much like Captain Cuffe, who had amassed a fortune by inventing a patented device for handling sails and becoming one of the major sail makers in Philadelphia. Like Cuffe, he, too, used his money to advance the cause of freedom and justice for African Americans. On the issue of the Back-to-Africa movement, Cuffe and Forten were on opposing sides.

The resolution the Philadelphia group drafted stated in part:

> "Whereas our ancestors (not of choice) were the first successful cultivators of the wilds of America, we their descendants, feel ourselves entitled to participate in the blessings of her luxuriant soil, which their blood and sweat manured; and that any measure or system of measures, having a tendency to banish us from her bosom, would

not only be cruel, but in direct violation of those principles, which have been the boast of this republic . . . "

Paul Cuffe never saw his dreams realized, because he died on September 9, 1817 at the age of fifty-eight. James Monroe, then the President of the United States, continued to be interested in the Back-to-Africa movement. On February 6, 1820, eighty-six blacks sailed from New York City on the *Mayflower of Liberia.* They arrived in the capital city of Monrovia on March 9.

But without the dynamic presence of Captain Cuffe, combined with the indifference of blacks, the Back-to-Africa movement lost momentum. The idea didn't die, however. It was resurrected again after World War I when Marcus Garvey built the Black Star shipping line to transport blacks from the United States to Africa and to establish United States trade with African nations. He was deported before his plans could be realized.

The legacy of Captain Paul Cuffe lived on. When he died, he left shares of his ship the *Traveller* to his daughters Alice and Rhoda, which made them among the few women shipowners in the country, and for several generations his sons and grandsons continued to be seamen and civil rights activists. Believing that one way to overcome racism was to provide leadership by being responsible and productive, Cuffe's family continued to look for ways to improve their lives and the lives of other free blacks. For example, Captain Cuffe's two sons spent most of their lives at sea. As the captain of the whaler *Rising States*, William Cuffe commanded an all-black crew. The ship was wholly owned by black investors. Paul Cuffe, Jr., spent thirty years at sea and later published a book about his many adventures.

Pardon Cook, the captain of three voyages of the whaling brig *Elizabeth*, was Paul Cuffe's son-in-law. The crew list of Cook's third voyage in 1841 on the *Elizabeth* shows that at age twenty-one he commanded both black and white men. Returning after a year, they had 260 barrels of spermaceti oil and 120 barrels of regular oil. On this voyage, Paul's nephew, Asa Wainer, was Cook's first mate. Paul Wainer, Asa's father, had served as the captain of the *Protection* between 1821 and 1822.

The Cuffe name was thereafter associated with excellence, success, and courage. But the year after Captain Cuffe died, a slave boy was born in Tuckahoe, Talbot Country, Maryland. His name was Frederick. He escaped slavery and changed his last name to Douglass. In 1841, while Absalom Boston was fighting for his daughter's right to attend an integrated school on Nantucket, Frederick Douglass, a caulker of whale ships, was on the threshold of becoming one of the most celebrated black leaders in the world.

FREDERICK DOUGLASS AT NANTUCKET

The militant abolitionist William Lloyd Garrison called for the conference of the Massachusetts Anti-Slavery Convention to meet on Nantucket at the Atheneum on August 11, 1841. Frederick Douglass was scheduled to speak.

Douglass was unknown before that day. As far as anybody knew he was a runaway slave from Maryland who was making a living as a ship's caulker in New Bedford. He had never made a speech before.

He began by saying, "You have come here to learn about slavery. I stand here before you as a graduate of the peculiar institution with my diploma written on my back."

When he finished, his audience was deeply moved and they applauded long and hard, knowing that this was his first public address, but not his last. In time they came to know the details of this great orator's life.

Douglass gave full credit to a seaman named Benny, who had helped him escape. Frederick was born a slave in Maryland, in February 1818. His master's wife,

Two hundred years ago, 700 whaling ships were registered to whaling centers such as New Bedford and Nantucket. Here, a whaleman prepares to harpoon a whale. [New Bedford Whaling Museum]

Escaped slaves and free blacks often chose to work on the notoriously dangerous whaling ships. This painting was created by an unknown whaleman. [New Bedford Whaling Museum]

PROTECTION.

No. 1613.

United States of America.

STATE OF MASSACHUSETTS.   DISTRICT OF NEW-BEDFORD.

I *Lemuel Williams*  Collector of the District aforesaid,
Do hereby certify, That *Israel White*
An American Seamen, aged *Thirty seven* years, or thereabouts, of the height
of *5* feet *9½* inches, *black* complexion, *nully* hair, *black* eyes,
born at *Little Creek*

Delaware

has this day produced to me proof in the manner directed in the Act entitled " An
Act for the relief and protection of American Seamen," and pursuant to the said Act,
I do hereby certify, that the said *Israel White*
is a **CITIZEN OF THE UNITED STATES of AMERICA.**

In Witness Whereof, I have hereunto set my hand and
Seal of Office, this *25th* day of *November*
in the year of our Lord one thousand eight hundred and
thirty. *Six*.

Lemuel Williams Collector.

*Sailor's Protection Certificates were issued to protect seamen from being forced
into service by the British. This one was issued to Israel White at New Bedford,
Massachusetts, in 1836. [The Kendall Whaling Museum]*

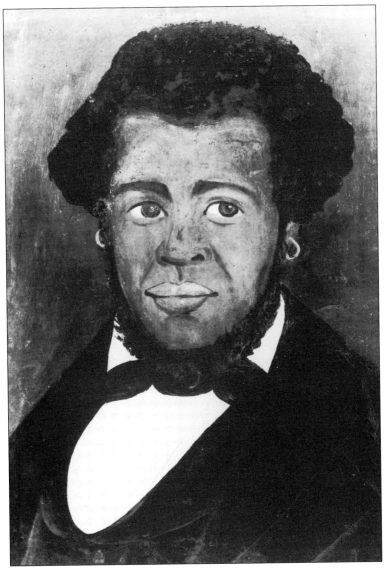

Absalom Boston was the captain of an all-black whaling ship. [Nantucket Historical Association]

By the time he was twenty-five, Paul Cuffe (sometimes Cuffee) owned and captained his own ship. Eventually, he used his ships for trade with Europe and Africa. [Schomburg Center for Research in Black Culture]

Capt. PAUL CUFFEE, a man of colour is about to proceed to Africa, with several families to form a settlement there. He will sail in the brig Traveller, now at Philadelphia, receiving two families there—afterwards touch at New Bedford and receive the remainder of her company, and proceed the latter part of October on her voyage.

In 1816, Captain Cuffe transported thirty-eight free blacks to Sierra Leone in West Africa. Many black communities didn't agree with Cuffe's idea that going back to Africa was the only way for blacks to be truly free. [State Historical Society of Wisconsin]

William Lloyd Garrison called for a conference of the Massachusetts Anti-Slavery Convention on August 11, 1841. It was the first time that Frederick Douglass would speak publicly. [Courtesy Chicago Historical Society]

INTERESTING COURSE OF LECTURES

TO SUIT THE TIMES,

AT CONCERT HALL.

THE EXECUTIVE COMMITTEE

OF THE

Social, Civil, and Statistical Association,

OF THE COLORED PEOPLE OF PENNSYLVANIA,

Viewing the great changes going on with regard to their race, feel deeply impressed that rare opportunities at the present time present themselves for accomplishing a very great amount of good, by a course of lectures in this city from able advocates, (white and colored,) of equal rights and universal freedom.

As oppression has ground down the slave of the South, so likewise does prejudice and proscription weigh heavily upon the free colored man of the North; therefore, whatever tends to remove these evils, aids in elevating the race; hence, with the hope of removing prejudice in a measure, by properly enlightening the public mind, these lectures have been gotten u p.

The speakers engaged for the course, are as follows:

WM. LLOYD GARRISON,　　J. M. LANGSTON. ESQ.,
REV. SELLA MARTIN,　　FREDERICK DOUGLASS,
F. E. WATKINS HARPER,　　HON. WM. D. KELLEY.

Of the ability of the speakers, and their deep interest in the cause, it is needless to speak. The Committee hope the well-known reputation of the speakers, and the good cause for which they are to speak, will ensure the full success of their efforts.

The proceeds to go to the Association to aid in procuring the Rights of Colored People on the City Passenger Railways, or to aid the freedmen, or sick and wounded soldiers.

MR. GARRISON,

WILL DELIVER THE OPENING LECTURE

On Monday Evening, January 16th, 1865,

HIS THEME WILL BE

THE GUILT, PUNISHMENT AND REDEMPTION OF OUR COUNTRY.

The time for the subsequent Lectures, &c., will be duly announced in the daily papers.

Tickets 25 cents to each Lecture,

May be had of T. B. PUGH, Sixth and Chestnut, or of any of the undersigned Committee, and at the door.

ISAIAH C. WEARS,　　U. B. VIDAL,　　MOSES WHEELER,
JACOB C. WHITE, Sr.,　　HENRY GORDON,　　WM. P. PRICE,
JONATHAN C. GIBBS,　　CHARLES H. BISTILL,　　MORRICE HALL,
STEPHEN SMITH.　　REDMAN FAUCET,

WM. STILL, *Chairman of Committee of Arrangements.*

A handbill for a series of lectures at which William Lloyd Garrison and Frederick Douglass spoke

In February 1818, Frederick Douglass was born a slave in Maryland. [AP/Wide World Photos]

A lithograph of New Bedford, Massachusetts, in the early 1800s [Claire White-Peterson Photo, Mystic Seaport, Mystic, Connecticut]

The Fugitive Slave Act of 1850 called for the use of federal officers to catch runaways. [New York Public Library]

Sophia Auld, taught him how to read. When she learned that it was against the law to educate a slave, she stopped, but by then it was too late. "A man who can read is not likely to remain a slave," Douglass said many times. He was determined to run away to freedom.

In 1838 Baltimore was a city divided — half slave, half free. Hugh Auld, Frederick's master at the time, hired him out as a ship caulker. One day at lunchtime, Frederick met Benny, a free black sailor whose ship had sailed without him. It didn't seem to bother Benny, for he had made up his mind to stay in Baltimore for a while. Frederick helped him get a job at the shipyard.

Benny introduced Frederick to other free blacks who were living in Baltimore at the time. He was asked to join the East Baltimore Mental Improvement Society. Most of these young men and women were free people who could read and write. Frederick fell in love with a young woman named Anna Murray. But he wouldn't marry her until he was free.

On September 2, 1838, Frederick decided to put his plan to escape from Hugh Auld into action. Dressed in Benny's sailor's clothing — a white shirt, red scarf, dark pants, and a tarpaulin hat, he used Benny's sailor's protection papers to board a train. He bought a ticket from the conductor, holding his breath until after the conductor had examined the identification. If the conductor had looked closer, he would have realized that the person described looked nothing like the man before him — Frederick, the runaway.

Later on, when he spoke, Douglass kept his audiences on the edge of their seats with the story of the slow progress of his train ride. Mile by mile, they followed the train as it crossed into Delaware, which was still a slave state. Douglass had to be very careful. At Wilmington, Delaware, he took a steamship up the Delaware River to Philadelphia. There his sailor's protection papers were checked again, but not closely. From Philadelphia, Frederick took another train and arrived in New York on Tuesday, September 4, 1838. Freedom!

Just as he had promised, Douglass sent an important message to Anna Murray. She rushed to New York, where they were married immediately. The couple then moved to New Bedford where Nathan Johnson (1822–87), a well-known African-American member of the Quaker Society of Friends, helped Douglass find work caulking whalers.

Douglass soon began attending abolitionist meetings and became an active member of the Anti-Slavery Society. William Lloyd Garrison took an interest in

Douglass and invited him to speak at an antislavery convention on Nantucket in 1841.

He was invited to speak again the following year. Returning to Nantucket in 1842, he was an experienced speaker, forceful and dramatic. But the tone of the other speakers' speeches was more strident and confrontational. Stephen Foster (not the composer) accused the clergy of being "a brotherhood of thieves . . . pimps of Satan," because they didn't take a more active stand against slavery. An attack like this was considered blasphemous even by Nantucket's liberal standards.

Angered by the speeches regarding the clergy, some people threw bricks through the building where the meeting was being held. Unfortunately, a woman was wounded when she was hit in the head. The atmosphere on Nantucket in the 1840s was very different from what it had been two decades earlier.

In the audience that night was no doubt Absalom Boston, who had been the captain of his own ship, yet his daughter was not accepted in public schools. And there was Reverend Arthur Cooper who, like Douglass, had been a runaway himself.

In 1820, Arthur Cooper and his wife Mary had escaped from Virginia on a sloop headed for Nantucket. They'd joined the black community there, set up housekeeping in a house on Pleasant Street, and began a family. Two years later, agents from Virginia came to the island, claiming that the Fugitive Slave Law gave them the right to return the Coopers and their infant daughter, born on Nantucket, to their master. In defiance of the law, black and white Nantucketers formed a line to block the slave hunters from entering the Coopers' house. This stalling tactic, allowed others to help the Coopers dressed as Quakers escape out their back door. They were hidden in several houses until the slave hunters gave up and left the island. Mary Cooper died four years later.

Arthur Cooper, like Frederick Douglass, could have lived a quiet, peaceful life in freedom, but he chose to take a stand against slavery. He became a leading citizen, serving as the pastor of the newly organized African Methodist Episcopal Church (known as Zion Church) and an outspoken abolitionist.

Pro-slavery supporters accused Douglass of being a fraud, because he was "too literate" and "too articulate." To counter their accusations, Douglass wrote his first autobiographical work, *Narrative of the Life of Frederick Douglass, an American Slave*, giving names, dates, and places that verified his story.

To keep from being reenslaved, he fled to England

where slavery had been abolished, and rejoined his family in Buffalo, New York, only after two friends had purchased his freedom. Douglass used money he had earned as a speaker in England to begin a newspaper called *North Star*, first published on December 3, 1847. And from then on, Douglass dedicated his life to freedom, justice, and equal rights for all citizens, including women. He returned to Nantucket five times as a visiting speaker.

Change was in the wind, and times were changing rapidly on the island of Nantucket. On July 13, 1846, at 11:30 p.m., a fire started in a Nantucket hat shop and rapidly spread to the wharves. The whale oil ignited and everything burned — oil, sails and rigging, buildings. Even the ships were engulfed in flames.

At the same time as this disaster, the sperm and right whales had been hunted to the brink of extinction in Atlantic waters — from the Americas to Africa. The whalers pursued their prey into the Arctic. Then whales were discovered in the Pacific, but to make the journey all the way around the tip of South America was long and dangerous, so larger ships were built and larger crews were required.

The newer ships were too big to enter Nantucket's shallow harbor, so they began going into New Bedford.

After the fire, there was no need to rebuild; it was easier for businessmen to move to New Bedford on the mainland, as several of them had already done.

Whale ships would continue to sail from Nantucket's harbor for many more years, but it was never the same as before the great fire. A majority of young men were no longer looking to the sea for their fortunes, but to the gold fields of the West. The fire devastated businesses but the drop in population was even more damaging.

The glory days of Nantucket whaling were over, but never forgotten. The island still thrives as a tourist center where Americans can come to get a glimpse of a time when black hands raised white sails that caught the winds that carried them far out to sea.

CHAPTER FOUR

NEW BEDFORD

NEW BEDFORD 1848

In 1848 New Bedford was a bustling town full of energy, growth, and daring. It quickly became the center of the abolitionist movement and a dominant whaling port.

There were about 700 blacks living in New Bedford in 1850. That number does not include Cape Verdeans, who insisted upon living in their own neighborhoods. The city directory shows that a large number of African Americans were seamen on whaling vessels. And there is substantial evidence that shows black-owned businesses in New Bedford were among the most successful in the country. Quaker whaling seemed to be a winning business for blacks in New Bedford, just as it had been in Nantucket. And the coalition between blacks and Quakers helped make New Bedford a center for the abolitionist movement.

It is not surprising that New Bedford was a major station on the Underground Railroad. Even today, New Bedford residents are proud of their antislavery heroes. Plaques and historical markers honor the men and women, blacks and whites, whaling captains and ordinary seamen, who used their attics, cellars, farmhouses, and idle ships in harbor to assist runaways who were bound for Canada.

Most runaways took to the sea as soon as possible. And even though it was illegal to knowingly accept a runaway as a crew member, there were plenty of shipowners who did. A letter written by a runaway on board a whaler in the Pacific and printed in the annual report of the American and Foreign Anti-Slavery Society told about his escape from Louisiana to Brooklyn, New York. Although he found a job in Brooklyn, he didn't feel safe enough, so he shipped out on a whaler. "I fled," he wrote, "from Brooklyn because I could not sleep, as I was so near the slaveholding country. I thought I could not be safe until I had gone to the other side of the globe."

Another slave took refuge on the *Cornelia* in New Bedford. The captain discovered the runaway and turned him over to the authorities. A free black who had helped him was given a prison term. As it turned out the father of the captain was Joseph Ricketson, a longtime supporter of the antislavery movement. He wrote an open letter in *The Liberator* on January 24, 1845, in which he criticized his son, saying he "would much rather have the vessel jeopardized or even lost forever" than be "involved in the recapture of a slave and the loss of a free black's freedom on account of it."

Men like Captain Daniel Drayton, captain of the *Pearl*, were rare. He helped smuggle slaves out of Virginia to freedom, working in connection with William and Luanda Bush, who were conductors on the Underground Railroad in Washington, D.C. Unfortunately, Drayton was caught and imprisoned for his involvement, but the Bushes fled to New Bedford where they continued their work as conductors. After his release from prison, Captain Drayton also returned to New Bedford. Years after his death, the Bushes' grandson, Andrew Bush, erected a monument in memory of Captain Drayton in New Bedford.

The Fugitive Slave Act of 1850 called for the use of federal officers to catch runaways. This infuriated abolitionists, and even neutral New Englanders who had been critical of men like Garrison were moved to action. Empowered by the Fugitive Slave Act, slaveholders or their agents actively pursued runaways, by soliciting help and offering rewards to those who had information.

Slaveholders also used posters to discourage individuals from helping fugitives in their flight to freedom. Newspaper ads about runaways appeared regularly in columns next to ship crew calls, and shipowners, captains, and ordinary seamen were admonished that violators would face "the severest penalties of law."

Still, runaways flocked to New Bedford, where they knew there was plenty of support. In an interview with a reporter in the 1920s, Joseph M. Smith described how he had escaped from slavery in the 1850s. In recalling what happened, Smith said he had stowed away on a lumber ship sailing from North Carolina to New Bedford. "I waited until the captain went down below to dress for going ashore, and then I made a dash for liberty. I was over the edge in the midst of an excited crowd. 'A fugitive. A fugitive!' someone cried. But a slave had little to fear in a New Bedford crowd in slavery days. They stood aside and let me pass."

Henry "Box" Brown paid a friend 169 dollars to ship a crate from Richmond to Philadelphia. Brown was hiding inside and endured the twenty-six-hour trip. Via the Underground Railroad he was brought to New Bedford, where he was given a hero's welcome.

At the corner of William and Purchase Streets in

New Bedford there is a plaque commemorating Rodney French, the community's mayor who in 1851 had rung a bell to warn hiding slaves that federal agents and slave owners were coming by ship into the New Bedford harbor. A newspaper report dated April 22, 1851, stated, "We are pleased to announce that a very large number of fugitive slaves, aided by many of our most wealthy and respected citizens, have left for Canada and parts unknown."

SLAVE SHIPS STILL RUNNING

Given its history, it isn't surprising that New Bedford was the center of a lot of abolitionist sentiments. But there were also ships coming in and out of New Bedford that were involved in the slave trading business.

In 1808 the importation of slaves from the west coast of Africa was prohibited by the United States. But there is documentation that slave trade continued up until 1859 when the last slave ship, the *Clothilde*, brought a shipment of slaves into Mobile, Alabama.

Since whaling vessels could be easily outfitted as slave ships, New Bedford was a logical place for slavers to set up operation. Who would suspect them in the bosom of Yankee abolitionists? Even though there were plenty of inspectors armed with the authority to shut down any such illegal operations, it was hard to catch them. No shipowner was likely to admit that he was breaking the law.

By 1859, however, there was a major crackdown on slaving vessels that operated out of northern ports. For example, in early 1859 a New York vessel was prevented from coming to New Bedford to be outfitted as a slaver. The *Memphis*, a merchant ship, left New Bedford in February 1859 for the Indian Ocean, but it was reported to have been seen in Cuba later that year delivering a cargo of African slaves. Also in 1859, the *Brutus* left on a whaling voyage. Two years later the owners were indicted in Boston for slave trading. The *New York Post* published the names of eighty-three ships that were seized for slave trading. Over twenty were registered as whalers.

THE SEAPORT

Author Irwin Shapiro gives a good view of New Bedford as a seaport: "Tall-masted ships crowded the harbor, and the wharves were lined with casks of oil giving off a heavy sweet smell. Merchants in high silk hats and long-tailed coats picked their way across the oil-soaked ground. They checked their cargoes and gave orders to workmen, who covered the casks with seaweed to protect them from the weather."

On the waterfront was an assortment of buildings — ". . . banks, the insurance companies, the law offices, and warehouses, oil refineries, and shops of dealers in oil, bone, and spermaceti. All were connected with whaling."

Farther away from the wharves, away from the smell of the ships, were the houses of the wealthy shipowners, captains, and merchants. Here and there were taverns where young seamen of every nationality could be found laughing, singing, and swapping whale tales.

On top of Johnny Cake Hill stood the Seaman's Bethel, a church for whalemen. It was nondenominational and all seamen were welcomed and encouraged to thank God for their safe return or ask for God's protection during their upcoming voyage. The sermon of Jonah was a favorite text among seaport ministers.

LAND SHARKS AND WHARF RATS

New Bedford's whaling industry provided jobs for people in a variety of supporting businesses and crafts. While many did their business honorably, many of them didn't.

Signs advertising room and board were everywhere. Anyone who had an extra bedroom rented it out, because sailors always needed a place to stay while waiting for their ships to sail. The second floors of many commercial buildings were converted into sailors' quarters.

The greed associated with sailors' boardinghouses was overwhelming. Except in rare occasions, the rooms were dirty, the beds dirtier still, and the food, if not rotten, was unrecognizable. Sailors often had to share quarters with several other men and a few rats, who ate as much as the men but paid nothing. When the poor sailor left he probably took along an infestation of body lice or another more serious disease. All of this for the highest prices in town.

There are alarming stories about young men who woke up from a drunken sleep, only to find that their landlord had shipped them out on a whaler, for which the unscrupulous man or woman had been paid a "finder's fee." These human leeches exploited their customers and robbed them of everything they had, including their clothing; in some cases they murdered them. James Dyre ran such a house in New Bedford. His place was so squalid and filthy, cholera broke out and killed those who lived there.

Jimmie Axum earned enough money as a seaman to open a boardinghouse in Providence. Instead of being more sympathetic to his brethren of the sea, Axum had a reputation for stripping his customers of their money and their lives if they didn't give their money over willingly.

But there were also genuinely good men such as William P. Powell, who maintained the Sailors' Temperance Boarding House in New Bedford during the late 1830s. Later, Powell, an African-American Quaker, opened Golden Farm, a retirement home for sailors located in New York City, and he also started the first Seamen's Union.

By all reports his quarters were clean, reasonably priced, and safe. But, any sailor staying with Powell had to be prepared for his endless lectures about self-improvement and the avoidance of drinking, gambling, and prostitution. And as a founder of the Manhattan Anti-Slavery Society, he tried to persuade black men to actively participate in the abolitionist movement. Powell brought in guest speakers and of course he collected money from the sailors to aid the movement and the continued work of Frederick Douglass and William Lloyd Garrison.

Powell was an exception and so were the men who stayed with him, for most sailors would have rather lived with fleas and roaches than give up drinking, gambling, and women.

Down on the wharves near the ships, "outfitters,"

known as land sharks, sold socks, shoes, and other clothing. These merchants, with their toothy smiles, met all arriving ships, hoping to be the first to catch the newly paid sailors.

There were also talented and very legitimate craftsmen, many of them African American, whose work was outstanding, including coopers, sail makers, riggers, rope makers, carpenters, chandlers, and blacksmiths. Lewis Temple, for example, was an African-American blacksmith who made a very important contribution to the whaling industry.

LEWIS TEMPLE

Very little is known about Lewis Temple's early life. He was born in Richmond, Virginia, in 1800, the year Gabriel Prosser led a rebellion in that city. His parents were probably emancipated slaves who moved to New Bedford, or he came to New Bedford on his own.

By 1836 Temple had his own blacksmith shop on the waterfront. There he often heard the whalemen talking about how easily their harpoons pulled out of the whale once it had been struck. Temple developed a "toggle" harpoon with barbs that stuck into the whale's body and wouldn't pull out easily. Temple changed the design of the harpoon forever.

But Temple didn't patent his invention, so other blacksmiths copied and sold his specially designed toggle harpoon. Still, the whalemen who used the harpoon knew who was responsible for it and named it the Temple Toggle iron. Temple died in 1854, and his son Lewis Temple, Jr., became a well-known businessman.

JOHN MASHOW

In New Bedford's harbor, vessels of many sizes rested from their long journeys or waited patiently to set sail. Birds squawked and fussed with one another over bits of garbage and food as the great masts groaned and moaned.

Those who knew ships could easily point out what kind they were by their rigging. Rigs were the masts, spars, ropes, and sails that drove the ship, and the arrangement of the masts and sails denoted whether the vessel was a ship, bark, brig, schooner, or sloop.

Whalers were usually rigged to be brigs, barks, or ships, as all three-masted, square riggers were called. Clipper ships were sleek and graceful, built for speed and agility. By contrast, the whaler was a big hulk built for endurance. Along the sides were whaleboats that were hung on wooden brackets. On deck was the tryworks, a brick furnace equipped with cast-iron pans that were used to boil the blubber into oil. Below deck were the captain's quarters in the rear of the ship, and the crew's quarters located forward in the forecastle.

John Mashow knew a whaler like a race car driver knows his automobile. That's why he could design and build them so well. He is credited with having crafted over one hundred ocean vessels, including sixty whalers and merchant ships.

Born in 1805 in Massachusetts, Mashow was a free black. He began building ships at the age of twenty-five, and since shipbuilders usually retained, as partial payment, a share in the vessel they built, Mashow quickly became a successful businessman. Records indicate that Mashow eventually held shares in seven ships.

Mashow's first whaleship was the *Nimrod*, built in 1841 in Dartmouth near New Bedford. For over thirty years he received glowing praises from whaling captains, owners, and crew who said his ships were among the best in the water. The names of these vessels are part of nautical history and include the *Cape Horn Pigeon*, the *Morning Light*, the *Sea Queen*, the *Henry H. Crapo*, the *A.R. Tucker*, the *Benjamin Tucker*, the *Elliot C. Cowden*, and the *Matilda Sears*, which made five whaling voyages.

Mashow had to know different woods and understand how and in what capacity they functioned best. He knew, for example, that oak formed the skeleton of the ship. Cedar made the best planking, but fir cleaned well and was therefore used for the decks. Pine framed the keels and some planking. Mahogany and teak were used for trim, joiner wood, and finish carpentry, and ash was used for the boats' oars.

Every whale ship was equipped with boats that were used to chase the whale on the water. These boats were generally about thirty feet long, pointed at both head and stern, and built of light material. They were pulled by two sets of seventeen-foot oars and one steering oar approximately twenty-two feet long. Each whaleboat carried a sprite (spirit) sail that was used to sail back to the main ship when they were separated.

CHAPTER FIVE

WELCOME ABOARD

THE CREW

Most whaling ships leaving New Bedford in the 1850s had a crew of about twenty-five to thirty men, including the captain, officers, cooks, steward, craftsmen, and regular seamen.

Besides African Americans, New Bedford had a large population of other seamen of color who served on whale ships. Ship records show there were Afro-Portuguese from the islands of Cape Verde, the Azores, and other islands off the coast of Africa; Native Americans; Caribbean blacks; Latin American Indians; Maori from New Zealand and Australian aborigines; Pacific Islanders; and Malayans. Even though people from within these groups tried to maintain their cultural identity, whites persisted in lumping them all together under the category of "colored people."

Among the various groups who came to New Bedford on the whaling ships, the Cape Verdeans had the largest and most enduring impact on the seashore communities of New Bedford, Mystic, Providence, and others.

CAPE VERDEANS

The Cape Verde Islands are located 385 miles off the coast of present-day Senegal in West Africa. They were claimed by the Portuguese in 1441. During the peak of the slave trade in the seventeenth century, the Portuguese set up plantations and brought in African slaves to work the land.

The Portuguese men fathered children by African women who had come to the islands as slaves. A population of mulattos resulted. The new generation of Cape Verdeans was a racially mixed people who developed their own unique language, Crioulo.

During the whaling period, whale ships frequently stopped off at the Cape Verdean Islands to take on water, fresh foods, and also other provisions. They could also take on new and often more willing crew members. Captains found Cape Verdean men to be strong, hard workers who were grateful to get off the island. More than a few whaling captains exploited them by paying them ridiculously low lays. Still,

Afro-Portuguese men came to the United States, where they settled in several New England whaling ports and where many of their descendants live today.

One such man who made his way to the United States on a whale ship was Antoine DeSant. DeSant was a Cape Verdean born in 1815. Not much is known about his childhood, but when he was about fifteen, a Yankee whale ship offered him an opportunity to escape the hardships of his island home. Due to his skill he advanced through the ranks to become a veteran whaleman, and by the end of his career he was a successful New London property owner and businessman.

DeSant made at least four voyages out of New London, Connecticut, on the ship *Tuscarora* between 1832 and 1837. He also showed up on the crew lists of the whalers *Clematis*, *Georgia*, and *Superior*.

DeSant was a literate man who left a personal logbook, dated 1850, of his service on the *Portland*. It was not a whaling voyage, but was bound from Boston to San Francisco. In the log he tells about the gold rush mania that was causing such a problem in the whaling industry. The log ends with the *Portland* in harbor, unable to leave because all the crew had been struck by gold fever and deserted. It was not uncommon during this period for ships to be abandoned in California harbors, while captains and crews went off to seek their fortunes in the hills.

Perhaps DeSant struck it rich, but more than likely he made his way back east once the dreams of quick money were abandoned. For by the end of 1850, DeSant was back in New London and had established himself in the waterfront district as a barber and grocer. He became a citizen in 1872 and died at the age of seventy-one.

Another Cape Verdean of fine reputation was Frank Rogers, who distinguished himself on a number of Arctic whaling voyages. He was highly praised by the Arctic explorer Charles Francis Hall, who benefited from Roger's navigational experience.

In the widening search for new hunting grounds, whalers had begun scouting Brazilian waters below the equator as early as 1800, picking up crew members from the Caribbean and South America. Eventually, whalers rounded Cape Horn, which triggered Pacific whaling.

According to one maritime historian, "The powerful shoguns of Japan had closed their port to all outsiders. The Arctic Circle and Bering Straits were great hunting grounds, but the climate was unpredictable and cold. South America was in turmoil in revolution and therefore too unstable." Therefore Hawaii was the most logical place to set up a Pacific whaling port.

The first Yankee whalers arrived in Hawaii in 1819. To a New England sailor Hawaii was as close to paradise as one could get and still be on earth. Sunshine, beautiful beaches, exotic foods, and friendly people made it a perfect place to stop for provisions. A little too perfect, because the rate of desertion tripled over the next thirty years. As with Cape Verdeans, Hawaiians or *kanakas* (the Hawaiian word for "person") were familiar with whaling and made excellent harpooners.

OPEN DOORS TO JAPAN

Officially, Japanese ports remained closed to Yankee ships, but slowly contact between Americans and Japanese took place. African-American whalers played a significant role in those early encounters.

Captain William Whitfield of the *John Howland* rescued a Japanese fisherman named Manjiro Nakahama and four of his companions in 1841. Captain Whitfield befriended Manjiro, who stayed on the boat and learned whaling from the captain and his mates, one of whom was a black man.

Manjiro changed his name to John Mung — or sometimes seen as John Manjiro — and settled in

Fairhaven, Massachusetts. While living with Captain and Mrs. Whitfield, he attended school and learned English. Eventually Manjiro returned to sea and after many hardships and adventures, he arrived home in Japan. There he became a teacher of English, navigation, and whaling. When the United States and Japan began their initial talks regarding formal relations, Manjiro served as an invaluable interpreter.

In a separate incident in May 1845, a black harpooner by the name of Pyrrhus Concer was on board the *Manhattan*. He helped rescue several shipwrecked Japanese fishermen. When they sailed into Tokyo Bay, they were greeted by swarms of people who came to greet the crew. They were particularly interested in Concer's dark skin.

CHAPTER SIX

ALL HANDS
ON DECK

A GREENIE'S FIRST VOYAGE

One historian wrote, "It was exceptional to find a man of thirty in a forecastle." Ship documents show that many of the regular seamen who sailed out of New Bedford were greenhorns, or "greenies." They were called that because on their first voyage out they were seasick and threw up until they turned green.

The average age for a whaleman was twenty-two. Even many of the captains had yet to see their thirtieth birthday. Greenies were usually teenagers who had probably heard some old mariner telling a romanticized version of his life at sea. The old salt probably hadn't mentioned that once the greenie signed up, he was in for the hardest three to four years of his young life. Or that his job had the highest death rate, second only to mining. A greenie stood the chance of dying from disease, accidental drowning, murder, or a whale attack. Yet there was never a lack of men willing to sign on a whaler. Boys as young as ten and twelve arrived in New Bedford every day, readily identified by their new short wool jackets, known as "monkeys."

Imagine being a runaway slave from Virginia who has just signed up on a Yankee whale ship, around 1852. All around you are people from every part of the world. An older seaman, a free black from Boston perhaps, takes you under his wing and promises to teach you "the ropes." Today, "knowing the ropes" is a term that means understanding how things operate in an unfamiliar environment, but in the Age of Sail the saying meant that a sailor knew how to climb the rigging and move among the sails with ease and agility.

After visiting the Seaman's Bethel together the two of you make your peace with whatever deity you worship. Then you hurry to the wharf where you find the location of your ship and report for duty. The wharf is a busy place where everybody is pushing, pulling, turning, or hoisting something. You push your way through the crowd and hop on board.

As the ship pushes away from the dock, the sailors wave at their friends and loved ones who have come to say farewell. If a greenie is lucky, he might have someone come to see him off, but more often than not, a runaway was glad to be leaving, putting as much distance between him and his master as possible. At the last moment, a few late sailors always leaped on board. And unfortunately some of them "missed the boat."

Greenhorns had to learn a new way of speaking. Right was no longer right, but starboard. Left was port. Front was bow, and back or rear was stern. A seaman's language and sayings were so colorful, people adopted them into their everyday language. Terms such as "hard and fast" and "high and dry" were originally sailor's expressions.

TEN COMMON SEA EXPRESSIONS
AND THEIR MEANING TODAY

Hand over fist means a rapid progression in a job or earnings, for example, to "earn money hand over fist." To a seaman it was the way in which he climbed the rigging (ropes) by placing one hand over the other over the other.

Hard and fast meant that a ship had run aground hard and was stuck fast. Today, it means any rigid rule or regulation.

High and dry was a ship that was dry-docked, out of circulation. Today, it means in a bad situation.

Mainstay is the name of a ship's main mast. Today, it is synonymous with support.

Making headway meant that a ship was moving forward unimpeded. Today, it means making progress.

On an even keel meant that a ship was so well-built that it was not lopsided, and that insured smooth sailing. Today, the term applies to something that is steady.

A ringleader comes from the custom used by sailors who wanted to complain to their captain. Since no one wanted to have his name at the top of the list, sailors wrote their names in a circle or a ring.

Over a barrel means in a helpless position, but it derived from the practice of putting sailors over a barrel to whip them.

Groggy comes from the seamen's word for a rum or whiskey drink called grog. A person who had drunk too much grog was said to be groggy — a wobbly state coupled with incoherent speech. Today, it simply means unsteady due to sleepiness.

Out to sea has the same meaning as out to lunch or out of it. But in sea language it meant a drifting ship, moving with no direction or heading.

While he was learning the language a greenie had to understand the order of command. The captain was the first and final authority on board ship. No questions asked. And the "I-didn't-know" excuse was unacceptable. Whether you liked the captain or not didn't matter — his commands were obeyed.

Disobedience was dealt with quickly and severely in order to maintain discipline. A captain usually resorted to the whip against those who broke the rules. Sometimes "all hands" were called on deck when the captain wanted to make a speech or administer punishment.

The captain's quarters were in the stern, or back of the boat. Ordinary seamen weren't allowed in that part of the ship. It was a compact but comfortable room, simply designed with a desk, maps, charts, a built-in bed, a chair, and his sea chest.

The mates were the officers, and each ship had at least two to four, depending upon the size of the crew. The first mate was the second in command, the second followed him, and so on down the line. Officers slept in staterooms opening off the main or forward cabin. But one of the best perks was the privilege to eat in the officers' dining room or main cabin along with the captain.

Midship was called "steerage" and that is where skilled craftsmen were quartered. Coopers, carpenters, cooks, stewards, and blacksmiths lived there. If the ship was small, they slept in the forecastle with the rest of the crew. Due to their rank, however, their bunks were closest to the hatch so they could get air.

The greenie was led to the bow of the ship where there was a triangular room known as the "forecastle." This was his home for the next three to four years, and he shared it with up to thirty men. The English author Samuel Johnson wrote, "A ship is worse than a jail. There is, in a jail, better air, better company, better conveniency of every kind." One look at a whaler's tight and stuffy crew quarters makes most people feel uncomfortable.

Each crew member chose a bunk or berth from a row of double beds that lined the walls. Those closest to the hatch were premium, but a greenie could buy one if he was willing to pay the man who had claimed it first. Stored under the lower bunks were sea chests, where sailors stored all their possessions. These "lockers" contained items such as clothing, a knife, a musical instrument, books, maps, charts, compasses, pictures of family or a loved one, keepsakes, gifts, and perhaps paper and pen or a journal.

JOURNALS AND LOGS

A personal journal or "rough log" was a day-to-day diary of an officer or crew member. From these entries life on board a whaler took on a more interesting, colorful, and realistic picture. Here, for example, is an entry from the journal of John Jones, a steward on the *Eliza Adams*:

SATURDAY THE 3D. COD FISH DAY

This day strong breezes from the westward Ship heading S. by W. Nothing but Goneys and birds in sight. This is Saturday night at sea, the night in which the sailors of olden times use to drink the health of sweet hearts and wives, them was the times we read of, times past and gone; now, instead, of the can of grog we have a filter full of cold water on the table, the look of which makes a fellow shiver and turn in as soon as possible, forgeting wives and everything else, so ends.

Grog refers to the British Royal Navy's mixture of rum, water, and sometimes lime juice. The word comes from the nickname of the man who instituted this daily rum ration in the 1740s. Admiral Edward Vernon, a family acquaintance of George Washington (after whom Washington named his Virginia estate, Mount Vernon), was known as "Old Grog" because of the grogram (coarse fabric) coat he habitually wore. Hence, the can of grog that often appears in seamen's songs and toasts refers to the beverage and the tin vessel in which the ration was distributed — grog.

Seamen's journals were filled with personal notes about missing home, their mother's cooking, officers' mistreatment, their worries and fears, as well as poetry and artwork. Here is a typical entry dated Tuesday, September 3, 1844:

> *"I do not know what to write and I only undertake it because I can't do anything else . . . for the last three or four months, I have looked for whales hard — pulled hard in the boats, worked hard on board — and have done next to nothing — which is hard — and now I am very homesick and can't get home, which is harder yet . . ."*

Charles Benson, an African-American steward on the bark *Glide*, wrote about his experiences in several journals. Toward the end of one journey, he expressed fear of what might have happened to his family while he had been away. Benson wrote, "When I get on shore & most to the house I always find myself trembling all over & some times so faint that I can hardly stand." Seamen's journals are filled with these kinds of concerns. It was quite common for sailors to return home and find that their loved ones had died, married, moved away, or fallen in love with someone else.

Benson was relieved to learn that his family was intact and that they were well. "I was sorry to find Charlie with sore eyes," he wrote, "also Sid is not in very good health, but on the whole they were all in much better condition than I expected to find them. Thank God for his goodness say I."

From Benson's journals during his long years at sea we get a glimpse of what life was like for a nineteenth-century whaleman.

The officers were responsible for keeping the ship's official logs. A "smooth log" was the officer's log that was written in ink and submitted to the captain. It contained the daily occurrences during the ship's voyage, and reports of punitive action, requests, complaints — anything the officer wanted to be part of the permanent records.

The entries, like the sailors' journals, were filled with

day-to-day information about the weather, an inventory of food and supplies, movements of whales, and good places to take on provisions. And it is from these journals that new territory was discovered, new lands were charted, and weather patterns learned. The weather patterns and data were studied to determine when it was best to sail and where. Sailors, of course, had their own way of reading the signs of the sea as indicated in a Biblical quote, frequently paraphrased by sailors everywhere: "Red sky at night, sailor's delight. Red sky in morning, sailors take warning."

Every captain's logbook told what the weather was and what the longitude and latitude were at the time of his entry. The "captain's log" was the official document of the voyage. In it the captain kept records of daily activities and information about the crew, their conduct, the vessel, deaths, illnesses, crimes, punishment, and desertions.

ANSWERING THE BELLS

Greenies were allowed a few days of seasickness the first few days out to sea, but after that they were expected to answer the bells. Ships' bells announced the passage of time in half-hour sequences of up to eight bells, which struck at the end of a four-hour interval known as a "watch." Eight bells were struck six times in a twenty-four-hour period: noon, 4 P.M., 8 P.M., 12 midnight, 4 A.M., and 8 A.M.

Every sailor was expected to stand watch, either the port watch or the starboard watch. While one watch was on, the other was off.

FIRST WATCH . . . . 8 P.M. TO MIDNIGHT

SECOND WATCH . . . . MIDNIGHT TO 4 A.M.
(GRAVEYARD OR CHURCHYARD)

MORNING WATCH . . . . 4 A.M. TO 8 A.M.

FORENOON . . . . 8 A.M. TO NOON

AFTERNOON . . . . NOON TO 4 P.M.

Then there were two "dogwatches" of two hours each.

FIRST DOG WATCH . . . . 4 P.M. TO 6 P.M.

SECOND DOG WATCH . . . . 6 P.M. TO 8 P.M.

During the dogwatches, when the men came on deck they told stories and "chewed the fat," a term we use today to mean talking with friends.

A hole was cut in the side of the water barrel so that it could only be filled halfway, thereby conserving water. While on duty, sailors were not allowed to congregate and talk, but they often took the opportunity to gather at the water barrel, also known as the scuttlebutt or butt, and exchange gossip and rumors — or scuttlebutt.

Neither black nor white seamen truly understood the scientific nature of the whale, but they talked about them endlessly. It was the one thing that bound them together, giving them a oneness of purpose, and they talked about them every day whether they were on ship or on shore.

Whalers talked about the size of the whale and which kind contained the most oil. They compared the habits and personalities of various whales, told tales about the meanest one they had ever encountered, speculated on the origins of the mysterious substance ambergris, argued about the best hunting ground, or how long a whale could stay underwater. Many of the facts cited in these discussions were the product of misinformation and not grounded in science or actuality.

NICKNAMES

Nicknames were used frequently. Sailors were called "Jacks," which suggests that, like the name, they were "regular" or "ordinary" seamen. "Tar" is another name for sailors, derived from the custom they had of waterproofing their pants with a coating of tar.

In seamen's language, sailors also had nicknames for people and things in their world, such as using "Jimmy" before a word. Jimmy Cane was a strong wind close to a hurricane. A Jimmy Duck was a nickname for a cook — one who prepared poultry well, and a Jimmy Bungs was the ship's cooper.

Sometimes the crew called an officer "Paul," based on the character from the British play, *Paul Pry*. Paul Pry was a busybody who snooped about looking for something to report. In their journals, sailors substituted Paul for another's real name if they wanted to write something unfavorable about him.

In sailor's slang Tom Pepper was another name for a liar. Tom Pepper was the seaman the imps ran out of hell for being an inveterate liar (some stories say he was a cheater).

SHIP SLOP AND SHOPPING

The ship's cook and steward were responsible for cooking for the captain and the crew and serving them. The captain and his officers were served in separate quarters. The crew was fed on the main deck from wooden tubs, known as "kids."

Very often sailors abandoned a ship at the first port if the food was bad, so a good cook on a whaler was as essential as good sails. But after the ship had been at sea for a week or two, the fresh fruits and vegetables were gone, then a few weeks later, the meat became stale and the moisture hardened the flour and rotted the potatoes. From then on, the cook had to rely upon dried foods to prepare the meals.

A favorite dish among sailors was "salt horse," made with dried and salted beef that was soaked in water to soften it, and served with rice, potatoes, or beans. On "Banyan days" — named after the Banian cast of Hindus, among whom it is forbidden to eat flesh — no meat or fish was served.

After a few months of hunting whales and rendering whale oil, the greenie's new clothes were in bad shape. His shirt was torn, his pants were slick with grease. If he didn't bring extra clothing with him, he would have to buy new items from the ship's slop chest at four times the cost. All that a sailor might need he could buy — trousers, flannel shirts, hats, tobacco, underwear, socks, neck scarves, belts, knives, needles, yarn, boots, and spoons. Money wasn't necessary, but a close record was kept and when he returned to New Bedford all expenses were taken from his lay.

After a few months out, the smell of the forecastle was as foul and rancid as the clothing, mixing a combination of tobacco, salt water, sweaty clothing, and whale blubber. In the midst of all this, sailors kept all manner of exotic pets, from pigs to parrots. Lice were a common companion to all sailors, even those who tried to practice some measure of hygiene. The stench was so bad, some of the men chose to sleep on deck in a bed made of coiled-up rope or canvas.

But this was home for many of them for the next four years.

SEA SUPERSTITIONS

Sailors were superstitious to the extreme and took all omens and signs quite seriously. Sailors loved the company of cats. It was common to have one or two on board to keep the mice and rat population under control. Black cats were thought to be special, but if one was killed, to a seaman that meant the worst kind of luck was coming. If a cat's tail was fluffy it was said to have "a gale in its tail" and the wind was sure to come up. Cats were so dear to sailors that they called small ripples of waves on an otherwise calm sea "cat's-paws."

The cat-o'-nine-tails was not loved but feared. It was a whip made of nine strips of leather with knots tied on the ends. When whipped it was like being scratched by an angry cat. The term "not large enough to swing a cat" is believed to refer to quarters so tight that a man with outstretched arms could not swing this terrible whip.

Part of showing a greenie the ropes was teaching

him all the sea superstitions and how to read the omens that brought good luck or misfortune to him, his mates, and his ship. For example, whistling in the wind was a sure way to bring bad luck, because whistling woke the Devil (or caught his attention) and that was sure to be trouble.

Birds were harbingers of both good and bad luck. The albatross is a seabird that was honored by mariners as a symbol of good fortune. But killing one, by intent or even by mistake, could cause grave problems. Storm petrels, said to be the souls of dead sailors, brought the message that a storm was on the way. And to kill one meant the soul of the sailor would come back and destroy the ship.

Greenies were warned that during a late night watch, mermaids and mermen and kelpies might try to charm them into jumping overboard to join them in their watery home. Phantom ships were also feared as harbingers of bad luck. If, while on watch, a young greenie saw St. Elmo's fire, he was told to turn his face, for if the flamelike light fell on him he would die soon. For the most part, however, the eerie light was considered a good sign or omen. In reality, it is only a static discharge that glows sometimes in stormy weather over the masts.

But the most feared specter was the Flying Dutchman for it was a sure harbinger of doom. In the most famous of all sea legends, a Dutch captain by the name of Vanderdecken (Van Dyke) blasphemed against God during a raging storm off the coast of South Africa. It was said that the Dutchman and his crew were condemned to wander the seas for eternity. Songs and stories have been written about the Flying Dutchman, but for a sailor to see the ghost ship meant his ship would soon sink.

If a whaleman lived life to the fullest, when he "deep-sixed," referring to the six-foot nautical fathom measurement of water depth, his soul rested in Davy Jones's locker, which was at the bottom of the ocean. Or he might gather at the "Fiddler's Green," the mariner's idea of heaven.

African-American whalemen believed that if they were born encased in a caul (a filmy covering), they were destined to know the future. It was also believed that to keep one in your possession was to guard you from drowning. Newspapers on both sides of the Atlantic advertised cauls. In his 1850 novel *David Copperfield*, Charles Dickens wrote, "I was born with a caul which was advertised for sale in the newspaper for the low price of 15 guineas."

SHANTIES

Singing was a very important part of every seaman's life. Greenies were introduced to the special songs of the whalemen known as whaling shanties or chanties. This ship log introduces one of the most commonly sung shanties, "Boony Laddy."

SATURDAY 17TH BLACK FISH DAY.

This day strong winds from the Northard and westard ship steering W. by S. At 11 A.M. took in the main top gallant sail and reefed the top sails. Nothing in sight all this day. Boony laddy heland laddy &c. No Obs.

Boony laddy heland laddy refers to a sea chantey, or shanty, with Scottish origins that can be traced to Arctic whale fishery in the eighteenth century.

Was you ever in Quebec?
Boonie Laddie Highland Laddie.
Loading timber on the deck
Boonie Laddie Highland Laddie.

This log entry was written by a white who recorded the song as he knew it, but the same song was sung by blacks on the docks of Mobile as they loaded cotton onto ships. "Quebec" was changed to "Mobile" and "timber" became "cotton."

Nowhere did African Americans contribute more to marine history than in sea shanties. Based on the "call and response" of slave spirituals and the repeated refrain of the blues, seamen adapted the same patterns for their songs.

It was often said among sailors that "a good song was worth ten men on a rope." Sailors sang work songs that helped them as they pushed, pulled, lifted, or hauled heavy items on board ship or on the docks, the same as they did on land.

As young men came to the coastal cities and shipped out they brought with them the songs of the backwoods, rivermen, lumbermen, and mountainmen. Sailors' shanties were the borrowed rhythms of workers who labored in the fields cutting cane, picking cotton, chopping tobacco, and working the docks. As they sailed around the world picking up people, the folk lyrics of Europeans, Cape Verdeans, Asians, Caribbeans, South Americans, and Pacific Islanders were combined with the tunes of American digging songs, war songs, and marches, which created a unique musical form, as original as African-American spirituals and blues.

Whalers had their own shanties, each with lyrics and a rhythm that fit the work they performed. African Americans and Caribbean blacks were responsible for quite a number of them.

The shantyman, or shanty leader, often "raised" the song, meaning he set the tempo. The lyrics usually contained references to women, loved ones, drinking, gambling, bad luck, good luck, weather, ships, whales, and real people living and dead. Practically all of them were snappy and filled with colorful language, albeit vulgar at times.

Famous for his shanties was a black cook by the name of "Doctor," who, according to historian A. Howard Clark, was called upon by his captain to "wake 'em up, Doctor" when the men were cutting out a whale.

Doctor would then sing, in the call and response of African and African-American field songs:

> *Oh, a dandy ship and a dandy crew*
> Crew: *Hi ho! My dandy, oh!*
> *A dandy mate and a skipper, too.*
> Crew: *Hi ho! My dandy, oh!*
> *Oh what shall I do for my dandy crew?*
> Crew: *Hi ho! My dandy, oh!*
> *I'll give them wine and brandy, too.*
> Crew: *Hi ho! My dandy, oh!*

A very popular pulling or pushing shanty among black crewmen was "Hello Somebody."

Somebody's knocking with a bloody big stick,
  Hello, somebody, hello.
It's dirty Dick from New Brunswick,
  Hello, somebody, hello.
Haul away an' make yer pay,
  Hello, somebody, hello.
Haul away for Saccaraooa Bay.

The rhythm of shanties helped seamen as they pulled, rowed, cut, or lifted.

Grog time of day, boys,
Grog time of day,
  Chorus: Huro, my jolly boys,
Grog time of day.

A shanty of West Indian origin is "Shallow Brown," also known as "Challo Brown," about a mulatto woman. Sometimes she represents a woman who is longed for:

O, I'm going to leave her,
Shallow-oh, Shallow Brown.

O, I'm going to leave her,
Oh, Shallow-oh, Shallow Brown.
Ship on board a whaler.
Shallow-oh, Shallow Brown.
Ship on board a whaler.
Oh, Shallow-oh, Shallow Brown.
Ye are me only treasure,
Shallow-oh, Shallow Brown.
I love ye to full measure,
Oh, Shallow-oh, Shallow Brown.

And at other times Shallow was a woman a sailor was glad to leave behind.

Come put me clothes in order,
Shallow-oh, Shallow Brown.
The whaler leaves termorrer (tomorrow).
Oh, Shallow-oh, Shallow Brown.
For ye are fat an' lazy,
Shallow-oh, Shallow Brown.
Ye nearly drive me crazy,
Oh, Shallow-oh, Shallow Brown.

In his book, *Shanties from the Seven Seas*, Stan Hugill wrote that shanties "were always associated with work and there was a rigid taboo against singing them outside the framework of work. To sing a shanty when there was no work involved could mean courting trouble." So when they weren't involved in work, the sailors sang ballads and songs about their loved ones back at home.

Some of these songs contained seamen's stories about a well-known ship and crew, or perhaps their own. The song called the "Whaleman's Lament" reflects the second thoughts some sailors had after being out for a year or so.

Twas on the briny ocean
On a whaleship I did go.
Oft times I thought of distant friends,
Oft times I thought of home
Remembering of my youthful days.
It grieved my heart full sore
And fain I would return again
To my own native shore.

Through dreary storms and tempest
And through some heavy gales
Around Cape Horn we sped our way
To look out for sperm whales.
They will rob you, they will use you
Worse than any slaves.

Before you go a-whaling boys
You had best be in your graves.

If I ever return again
A solemn vow I'll take
That I'll never go a-whaling
My liberty to take.
I will stay home
And I will roam no more
For the pleasures are by few my boys
Far from our native shores.

Most sailors' songs were merry, lighthearted and meant to cheer the spirits of men who were far away from home and feeling lonely.

Come all you young Americans
And listen to my ditty.
It's all about a whaling bark
That left New Bedford city.
The bark Gay Head is her name.
She's known both far and near . . .

Once a verse was sung, additional verses were added by anybody who wanted to join in. A songfest of this kind could go on for hours, accompanied by harmonicas, banjos, fiddles, tambourines, and even drums.

Captains encouraged the crew to share songs and stories. Having fun lifted morale, but sometimes jokes went too far and fights broke out. A black greenie was automatically a target, so it was to his advantage to stand up for himself right away. Building a reputation for being tough was a way to protect himself from bullies. "Any expression of pity, or any show of attention, would look sisterly, and unbecoming to a man who had to face the rough and tumble of such a life," one marine historian wrote. But defending oneself and being mean were two different things. No greenie ever wanted to be referred to as "a dirty dog and no sailor," so he watched the way he treated his fellow mates. These ten unpublished "whalemen's commandments" summarize the conduct a greenie was expected to follow.

1. Steal but not from a friend.
2. Lie but never about anything important.
3. Fight anytime you think you can win.
4. Run when you think you can't win.
5. Cheat before you get cheated.
6. Swear but never in front of a good woman.
7. Drink as much as you can hold.

8. Love as many women as you can catch.
9. Never tattle.
10. Never volunteer.

When sailors weren't singing, swapping tales, or playing practical jokes, they sometimes wrote in their journals or carved. Some men made model ships in their spare time or carved stories and adventures on sperm-whale teeth — an art known as scrimshaw.

SCRIMSHAW

Scrimshaw artists scratched their designs in whale teeth or whalebone, then traced over the design with ink. Sometimes they used the jawbone of a sperm whale or the baleen of a right whale to make useful and decorative items that ranged from napkin holders to chess pieces and handles for walking canes. Some whalers drew elaborate scenes from exotic places they had visited. Some did portraits of the captain, the ship, or fellow crew members. Sailors stored their artwork and sold it when they returned home or in ports when they were on shore leave.

While there are many examples of scrimshaw on display in whaling museums, it is often difficult to identify the race of the artisan because not all of the items were signed. There are pieces, however, that show African-American subjects, such as a well-known portrait of a black sailor.

SHORE LEAVE AND GAMMING

Captains put into port for provisions and repairs as often as they could, but sometimes months passed before they saw land. When a ship docked at a foreign port, the crew took shore leave, a welcome relief for men who had been penned up for months. Shore leave was a captain's nightmare, however, because the desertion rate was so high. Frequently ships returned with fewer than eight of the original crew members still on board. It wasn't a crime to "jump ship" on a whaler, but those sailors who left before the return forfeited their lay.

Greenies often jumped ship early, generally at the first stop, and made their way home on a returning ship. But those who took a liking to the sea stuck it out. There were always local recruits who were ready to sign on wherever a ship stopped, so whalers are partly responsible for the movement of people around the world. In 1850 it was not uncommon to find blacks, Native Americans, and Europeans living in Liverpool, Peru, Hawaii, Tahiti, even the Arctic. And people from every part of the world were seen walking the streets of New Bedford during the heyday of whaling.

While on shore leave, greenies needed the advice and sometimes the protection of older and more experienced crew members. Young sailors, away from home for the first time, were wild with excitement and eager to take in as much as they could with total abandon. Thus, the greenie was a perfect mark for unscrupulous people who took everything he had and left him "flapping in the wind like a sheet." The sheet in this expression meant the line that was fixed to the lower corner of a square sail. When a sheet was allowed to run free, the sails lost their wind and flapped and fluttered, thus making the ship uncontrollable. A sailor left "flapping in the wind" was in a rather helpless situation. Though young sailors were often victimized by their naïveté, just as many caused problems for the local establishments.

Trouble seemed to follow young sailors. Never willing to back down from a challenge, they fought at the drop of a hat. According to one ship's log, the captain noted that he could spot a greenie from a distance. He was usually the one with the fresh scar and the bruised eye. Sometimes a greenie ended up in serious trouble or in jail, so he "missed the boat" when it sailed.

Not all whalemen were boisterous brawlers. A few industrious whalemen spent time selling their scrimshaw, visiting friends, or seeing the local sights. Some of them went to tattoo parlors where artists decorated their bodies. Others pierced their ears or visited a sweetheart they had met on a previous leave.

If a ship docked in a slave state or another country where slavery was legal, Africans and African-American freemen and runaway slaves sometimes chose to stay on board ship rather than risk the chance of being captured or sold into slavery. Once the ship moved into the Pacific, African Americans felt relieved because the farther they moved away from Europe and the Americas, the safer it was for men of color. While on shore leave, black crew members sometimes became involved with abolitionists and helped to plan and carry out daring escapes.

The authorities of Charleston, South Carolina, were very uneasy about the number of free blacks, especially seamen, who came in and out of the city and regularly mingled with the slave population. After the Denmark Vesey rebellion plot of 1822 failed, because a house slave warned his master, the authorities in Charleston passed a Black Seaman's Act, which made it mandatory for black seamen to stay in prison while their ships were in Charleston Harbor. Although the act was found to be illegal, the practice remained in force until after the Civil War. The purpose was to prevent sailors from being effective conductors on the Underground Railroad. But the authorities failed to recognize that some white sailors were conductors, too. And according to author Jeffrey Bolster, ". . . white sailors occasionally put themselves at risk to subvert slavery by helping slaves flee." The arrest of Edward Smith is a good example of that.

On March 27, 1839, Charleston police arrested Edward Smith, a white steward on the brig *Columbo* out of Boston. He was accused of distributing antislavery pamphlets to black dockworkers, some of whom were free and others slaves. On May 11, a grand jury handed down a bill of indictment and a few days later he was found guilty of "seditious libel." Although he denied knowing that he had committed a crime, Smith was fined one thousand dollars and sentenced to a year in prison.

Shore leaves could be dangerous in more than one way. No matter how sailors spent their shore leave, when it was time to get back on board, many of them who made it back to the ship in time did so one step ahead of the law or an angry husband. It was not an exaggeration that "a sailor had a girl in every port."

Shore leaves were few and far between, but the next

best thing was "gamming." A gam was a visit between two ships that met at sea. After dropping anchor, the captain and crew visited the other ship and exchanged news from home. Sometimes they learned who had won the presidency months after an election. The crew enjoyed gamming for more personal reasons. First, a gam provided a break from the long and lonely solitude of the sea and, secondly, since a majority of the whale ships came from New England, everybody wanted to know what was happening there. Even bad news was welcomed, because it was better than not knowing anything.

Sometimes the captains were neighbors or related to a crew member on board the gamming ship. Real acts of faith were the letters that wives took to the harbor and gave to departing captains of whalers. Their hopes were realized when their letters miraculously caught up with their husbands, delivered during a gam in the Pacific Ocean.

Getting a note from home was as exciting as a holiday. Sometimes it was a year old by the time it was delivered, but a whaleman read it with no less interest, and usually it was read and reread until it fell apart. If the ship was on the way back to New England, whalemen quickly wrote letters and gave them to the captain to deliver once the ship reached New Bedford,

Nantucket, Martha's Vineyard, or wherever it was bound for. Knowing how lonely many of his crewmates were, the man who got a letter would read it out loud, and in this way everyone felt like they'd received a letter from home.

Captains and mates were no different from their men; they longed for information about their families, too. A captain and his mates were anxious to talk with men who were their social equals, and they eagerly shared information about the movement of whales, and warned each other about ports that were in upheaval. They shared the politics of the day and the effects of major decisions on the cost of oil and the whale oil business.

Free blacks with families had the same concerns, but runaways were curious about what was happening with emancipation. Had slavery ended? What was being done to bring it to an end? To a runaway the answer to these questions determined if he might be able to go back home. Many of his fellow runaway slaves were living in Canada and Mexico because of the strict Fugitive Slave Act passed in 1850. The questions were being asked by more people than ever before. Quakers and free blacks weren't alone in their struggle. Other Americans had joined them by this time. So there was something to be hopeful about. But Frederick

Douglass was beginning to fear that slavery would only end with violence.

A gam could last a few hours or several days. Spirits were usually high after a gam, but a few men who received bad news about their families were not to be consoled. The captain knew that during the next shore leave one or two men would desert the ship in an effort to get home. Others would stick it out, choosing to stay on and finish the voyage and collect their lay.

CHAPTER SEVEN

PACIFIC WHALING

THE WHALE HUNT

By 1818 sperm whales were harder to find along the eastern coast of South America. So new grounds needed to be discovered. By the mid-1820s whalers were making regular trips to Pacific waters. Daniel Francis in *A History of World Whaling* described the course that most Yankee whalers took after leaving New Bedford or some other New England whaling port. "After leaving home, usually later spring, [they] crossed the Atlantic to the Cape Verde Islands and the Azores, where they hunted whales and put in fruit, vegetables, fresh meat, and water. Riding the prevailing winds south back across the Atlantic, they sailed through the Brazil banks and around Cape Horn into the Pacific. As they moved north again up the coast of Chile, the snow-capped spine of the Andes was visible behind the low shore in the distance." An alternate route was to sail around the Cape of Good Hope in South Africa and into the Indian Ocean and on to Ceylon. Some captains headed for Australia and New Zealand, where whaling was particularly good in March.

"All these different routes," wrote Francis, "depended on many variables — currents, weather, the success each captain was having . . . The important point is that whalers did not wander aimlessly across the face of the globe hoping to come across their prey." Captains understood the migratory patterns of whales and at what time of year they would most likely be found in which ocean. It was the captain's responsibility to make sure that he and his crew were in the best possible position to enjoy "greasy luck."

Once the ship reached whaling grounds in the Pacific, for example, one of the watches was always aloft in the crow's nest.

The officers and crew checked the rigging and sails daily, and made sure that the boats were ready when a whale was spotted. Each whaleboat was equipped with rope neatly wound in wooden tubs, oars, a sail, a water keg, knives, and a flag for identification in case it was separated from the main vessel.

A whale was spotted when it came up for air and

blew water out of its blow hole or holes. The spray of water told the lookout what kind of whale it was and the direction it was headed. "There blows!" he yelled and pointed. William Fish Williams, junior officer on the whale ship *Florence*, wrote that "I never knew why most writers of whaling stories insist upon using the words, 'There *she* blows,' because there is no reason for saying 'she' any more than 'he' and either would be a word too many. The cry was always 'There blows' with the last word long drawn out."

The captain yelled back, "Where blows?" And the lookout gave the direction and pointed. The captain, then, gave the order to lower the boats.

Immediately the crew lowered the boats into the water and hopped in. An officer headed each boat and ordered the oarsmen to row as fast as they could. "Pull as though the devil were chasing you," was a familiar yell. The harpooner then took his position at the front of the boat, armed with a harpoon that was tied to 2,000 feet of line or rope.

According to the whaler Dean Wright, "To strike a sperm whale the whaleman endeavors to place his boat directly astern of him; or if that is not practicable, he gets right ahead, which is rather more dangerous to the boat and boat's crew than the other. By all means the boat must not be brought abreast of [the whale] or he is almost sure to see [it] and will avoid being struck by going down, or will go so fast as to prevent the boat from overtaking him."

Once the harpooner and the boat were in the right position the officer shouted the command, "Give it the iron (the harpoon)!" The injured whale either ran, sounded, or breached. Sometimes the running whale pulled the crew so far away from the main vessel that their boat was lost in foggy or choppy waters. Sometimes the whale breached and turned to fight its attackers just as the legendary Caldera Dick was known to do.

Every whaler knew the story of Caldera Dick, a huge sperm whale that was known as a fighter. Even though it had been harpooned many times, it attacked boats and snapped them like twigs with one blast of its tail. But, in the end, most whales were killed — even Caldera Dick.

Although a whale weighed tons, a dead whale floated, making it possible for the crew to handle it easily. Back at the ship, all hands moved quickly, because a bleeding whale drew sharks.

Rendering the whale began when the men hoisted it onto a platform that hung over the side of the main ship. Men with razor-sharp cutting tools, known as flensing knives, removed the "blanket" or the outer skin of the whale. Next, they sliced the blubber into manageable hunks of fat known as "horse pieces" and brought them on board. The sperm whale had a head that contained several buckets of spermaceti, so that was harvested.

Then the horse pieces were sliced into thin strips known as "Bible leaves." These were dropped into 300-gallon kettles set in a brick furnace on deck. The oil was skimmed off the bubbling blubber, cooled in copper tanks, and then placed into barrels and stored.

This was hard, dirty work, but to a whaleman it was "greasy luck" to make a clean catch with no losses and no injuries. And even though the heat from the furnace was stifling hot and the stench of the boiling blubber was revolting, the men sang shanties to keep themselves going.

Through the day and into the night, the furnace coughed up billows of smoke that blackened the white sails. The men were covered with grease and blood, and when the whale was tried out, the whalemen dropped in exhaustion or prepared themselves to answer to the call of "There blows!"

MOCHA DICK AND *MOBY DICK*

Every whale that put up a good fight was compared with other famous whales. One of the greatest sea stories ever told was written by Herman Melville. He was a greenie who, before he became a writer, served on board the *Acushnet* during 1841. Ten years later, Melville wrote the famous historical novel *Moby Dick*. And according to Frank Bullen, a former whaleman, "Melville seems to have spoken the very secret of the sea and to have drawn into his tale all the magic, all the sadness, all the wild joy of many waters. It is, in my mind, the most fascinating story of the sea ever written. Better still, in all its history, it is unimpeachably correct."

The main character in the novel is Captain Ahab, a man obsessed with killing a great white whale named Moby Dick. In the novel Melville takes a lot of time describing the *Pequod* (the ship), the crew, the hunt, the work, and the dangers of Yankee whaling.

Actually, *Moby Dick*, the novel, was based on several true stories. Of the greatest fighting whales in the Pacific, Mocha Dick was the most well known. He was a very large bull sperm whale that warred on Pacific whalers for more than fifty years, killing at least thirty men. J. N. Reynolds, who published *The Knickerbocker* magazine, wrote in the May 1839 issue an account titled "Mocha Dick: The White Whale of the Pacific" of how this ferocious whale was killed. Nineteen old irons were found embedded in the whale's body. Melville

While 90 percent of black Americans were confined to plantations, black whalers roamed the world. A Japanese artist painted these American whalemen in Japan in 1845. [New Bedford Whaling Museum]

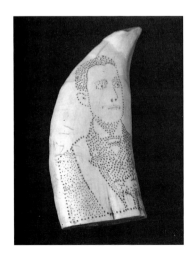

During long voyages, whalers often carved whale teeth or bones to pass the time. These carvings, which were traced over with ink, were called scrimshaw. [The Kendall Whaling Museum]

This crew list for the Acushnet *includes Herman Melville's name. Melville wrote the classic* Moby Dick *ten years later. [New Bedford Whaling Museum]*

Perched in the rings of a schooner, these two black sailors are standing watch. [The Kendall Whaling Museum]

After a whale was harpooned and killed, it was cut into manageable hunks of fat, then brought on board and sliced into smaller strips, which were boiled in kettles on deck. [Mystic Seaport Museum]

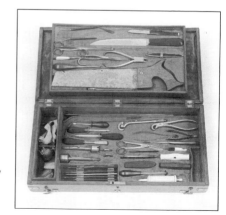

A ship's surgeon's chest [Courtesy Peabody Essex Museum, Salem, Massachusetts]

This photo shows ship caulkers at work in 1910. In 1838, Frederick Douglass was hired out by his master, Hugh Auld, as a ship caulker. [The Kendall Whaling Museum]

Captain Robert Smalls and his crew of slaves commandeered the Confederate gunboat Planter, putting her at the disposal of the Union navy. [Schomburg Center for Research in Black Culture]

My Full Name is *Sampson Dyer Pompey*
(Give all names in full)

I was Born at *Nantucket February 26, 1830*

Date of Birth

Name of Father *Stephen A Pompey*

Maiden Name of Mother *Trillonia Ann Dier*

If Married, When and to Whom? *14 day of September to Susan B. Kelley*

1875

Names of Wife's Parents *Richard A Kelley and Harriet B Kelly*

Date of Enlistment *September 6 1861 for one year*
(If enlisted more than once give each date)

Served in Co. , Regiment, State of *W.S.S Kingfisher Navy*   (Or similar data for other branches of the Service)

Rank at Time of Enlistment and Discharge *Odinary Seaman. Dis Able Seaman*

Engagements or Battles Participated in *cept After guard Port watch*

Date of Re-enlistment (if any)

Date of Mustering Out *Discharged in nov1862*

Remarks *We were kept two months ofer our time Stationed on the Blockade most of the time and Cruised in the gulf some*

(Signature in Full) *Sampson Dyer Pompey*

Born in 1830, Sampson Dyer Pompey, a black resident of Nantucket, served in the navy during the Civil War. [Nantucket Historical Association]

This photo shows the baby of Mate Gone, a sailor on the Wanderer. *[The Kendall Whaling Museum]*

When William T. Shorey reached the rank of captain in 1886, he was the only black captain in the New Bedford fleet. His wife, Julia, accompanied him on several voyages, but when their daughters Zenobia and Victoria were born, she chose to stay with them in San Francisco. [San Francisco Maritime National Historical Park, Victoria G. Francis Photographic Collection]

also drew from Owen Chase's *Narrative of the Most Extraordinary and Distressing Shipwreck of the Whale-Ship* Essex, the true story of a whaling vessel that in 1820 was run down and sunk by an enraged whale. In all three sources — both fiction and nonfiction — Africans, African Americans, and other men of color played important roles in the unfolding drama.

THE *ESSEX*

The *Essex* of Nantucket, commanded by George Pollard, Jr., set out on a Pacific whaling voyage on August 12, 1819. Owen Chase was taken on as the first officer and it is from him that the tragic story of the *Essex* was told.

The ship made the island of Floros in the western Azores on August 30. Sixteen days later it was on the Isle of May, one of the Cape Verde Islands. By December 18 it had recrossed the Atlantic and sailed down the coast of South America. Rounding Cape Horn the ship ran into bad weather, but once it reached the Pacific it successfully hunted whales for over a year without incident.

Then on November 20, 1820, a group of whales off the leeward bow was spotted. "There blows!" the lookout called. Lowering the boats the men began the chase for greasy luck. One boat went after an eighty-five-foot bull sperm whale. They managed to get several harpoons into it, but the injured animal didn't run, sound, or breach. It turned and attacked the ship! Whales routinely smashed the small whale boats, but they rarely went after the main ship. The horrified crew watched as the whale rammed the ship with its head, then the wounded animal disappeared beneath the water.

Chase and his crew hurried to see what they could salvage before the ship sank. In Chase's own words:

"I cut away the lashings of the spare boat . . . The steward had . . . gone down into the cabin twice, and saved two quadrants, two practical navigators, and the captain's trunk and mine; all which were hastily thrown into the boat . . . with the two compasses which I snatched from the binnacle. He attempted to descend again, but the water by this time had rushed in, and he returned without being able to effect his purpose. The ship had filled with water, and was going down on her beams-end; we shoved our boat as quickly as possible . . . into the water, all hands jumping in her at the same time, and launched off clear of the ship. We were scarcely two boats' lengths distant from her, when she fell over to windward, and settled down into the water."

When the captain's boat returned, he was shocked and dismayed to see the condition of the ship. Chase reported what he had seen, but it took a while for the truth to register with the captain. He and his men were a thousand miles from any charted land. But they had their whaleboats and what they had managed to save from the ship — fresh water, a musket, nails, files, and other items.

They were in serious trouble, but as good seamen, they believed they had a chance.

The three boats pushed away from the ship early the next morning. The first boat consisted of the captain and seven men; the first mate, Chase, had six men in his boat, and the second mate's boat held seven men. Of those twenty men who rowed away from the sinking *Essex* that day, six were black men — Richard Peterson, Samuel Reed, Lawson Thomas, Charles Shorter, Isaiah Shepherd, and William Bond.

It was agreed among the officers that the three boats would try to stay together. And to preserve their resources, food and water were rationed. Hunger and thirst plagued them almost from the beginning.

On November 28 they were hit by a storm. "The night set in extremely dark and tempestuous, and we began to entertain fears that we should be separated," wrote Chase. "We, however, with great pains, managed to keep about a ship's length apart, so that the white sails of our boats could be distinctly discernable."

Then, the captain's boat was attacked by a shark or some other large fish. One of the men poked at it with a lance and drove it away. Days passed, hour by hour. They were surrounded by water, yet they couldn't drink it. The few swallows allotted each day were not enough to quench the men's agonizing thirst. Slowly the seamen's bravado gave way to fear and their hope turned to despair.

On November 30, the crew in Chase's boat killed a turtle and drank the blood, then cooked the meat inside its shell. "The stomach of two or three revolted at the sight of the blood," wrote Chase, "and they refused to partake of it . . . I took it like medicine, to relieve the extreme dryness of my palate, and stopped not to inquire whether it was anything else than a liquid."

Using all their resources, they dived under the boat and found clams stuck to the bottom. They devoured them, but still the nagging hunger persisted.

On the morning of December 18 the three boats spotted land — a small, uncharted island. They didn't know what lay ahead of them, but they landed hoping to find water and food.

On the island they found birds, birds' eggs, and clams and they ate their fill. "We enjoyed during that night, a most comfortable and delicious sleep, unattended with those violent cravings of hunger & thirst, that had poisoned our slumbers for so many previous ones." The island offered little else. There was a trickle of water oozing from one of the rocks, but it was not enough to sustain them, so the captain made the decision to continue in the boats. Three crew members decided to stay on the island — William Wright and Seth Weeks of Barnstable, Massachusetts, and Thomas Chappel of Plymouth, England. The other three boats sailed on.

On January 10, 1821, after six weeks adrift, second mate Matthew P. Joy died. "On the eleventh, at six o'clock in the morning, we ... consigned him in a solemn manner to the ocean."

On the twelfth the boats were separated during a storm. Chase and his men were alone and severely weakened. One man stole bread from Chase's locker and blamed it on "the black man," presumably Peterson. But Chase knew better and admonished the crew member for lying. Peterson was too weak to move. Owen offered Peterson his small ration of a swallow of water, but the sailor refused. "He was sensible of his approaching end," wrote Chase, "and was perfectly ready to die: in a few minutes he became speechless, the breath appeared to be leaving his body without producing the least pain, and at four o'clock he was done."

Chase remembered speaking to Peterson a few days earlier on the subject of religion "on which he reasoned very sensibly, and with much composure." Peterson had asked Chase to let his wife know his fate. They buried Peterson at sea the next morning.

Isaac Cole died on the thirtieth of January ". . . groaning piteously . . . in the most horrid and frightful convulsions I ever witnessed." Chase wasn't sure when the idea came or to whom it came first, but they decided among themselves to cannibalize Cole's body in order to survive.

On the morning of February 16 they were found by the *Indian*, whose captain was William Crozier of London, England. They had survived a four-month ordeal that few men lived to tell about. By February 25 they had arrived at Valparaiso, Chile, where Chase learned that the captain's boat had been picked up near the island of Santa Monica, also off Chile.

The captain shared what had happened in his boat. On the brink of starvation, they took desperate measures. As men died they consumed their flesh in order to stay alive. Three blacks in the third boat were cannibalized after they died — Lawson Thomas, Charles Shorter, and Isaiah Shepherd. On the captain's boat Samuel Reed was cannibalized and Owen Coffin the cabin boy was shot and his flesh eaten. On February 28 they had lost sight of the second mate's boat and it was never heard from again. William Bond was lost in the third boat and his fate is unknown.

Those who were left on the island were picked up by a British ship on the fifth of April. Though weak and near death, they had survived. Thomas wrote later:

The "want of water was the most severe, their only supply being from what remained in holes among the rocks after the showers which fell at intervals; & sometimes they were five or six days without any. On these occasions they were compelled to suck the blood of the birds they caught, which allayed their thirst in some degree; but they did so very unwillingly, as they found themselves much disordered thereby."

In all there were nine survivors of the ill-fated *Essex*; those rescued from the boats were: Captain George Pollard, Jr., Charles Ramsdale, Owen Chase, Benjamin Lawrence, and Thomas Nicholson, all of Nantucket.

Owen Chase became the captain of his own vessel, and retired after many other voyages. He died in 1869, but he was always aware that starvation was only an accident away, so he kept food hidden away in case of an emergency.

Captain Pollard returned to the United States and he, too, was given another ship to master, but he lost it off the Sandwich Islands. "I am utterly ruined. No owner will ever trust me with a whaler again, for all will say I am an unlucky man."

The crew list of the *Essex* and their fate: ("do" means the same, or ditto.)

CAPTAIN GEORGE POLLARD	1st Boat	survived
OBED HENRICKS	do.	put in 3rd boat/lost
BRAZILLA RAY	do.	died
OWEN COFFIN	do.	shot/cannibalized
SAMUEL REED (black)	do.	died/cannibalized
CHARLES RAMSDALE	do.	survived
SETH WEEKS	do.	survived on island
OWEN CHASE	2nd Boat	survived
BENJAMIN LAWRENCE	do.	do.
THOMAS NICHOLSON	do.	do.
ISAAC COLE	do.	died/cannibalized
RICHARD PETERSON (black)	do.	died
WILLIAM WRIGHT	do.	survived on island
MATTHEW P. JOY	3rd Boat	died
THOMAS CHAPPLE	do.	survived on island
JOSEPH WEST	do.	lost
WILLIAM BOND (black)	do.	do.

LAWSON THOMAS (black)	do.	died/cannibalized
CHARLES SHORTER (black)	do.	do.
ISAIAH SHEPHERD (black)	do.	do.

From Owen Chase's *Narrative of the Most Extraordinary and Distressing Shipwreck of the Whale-Ship* Essex.

MUTINY ON THE *GLOBE*

In February 1808, the *Topaz*, a New England whaler mastered by Captain Mayhew Folger, approached Pitcairn Island in the South Pacific. There the last of the *Bounty* mutineers, John Adams, was found. The *Bounty* is probably the best known mutiny story in sea history, but the *Globe* was the most horrific of the whaling ship mutinies, and William Humphries, an African-American steward, was part of the plot.

The *Globe* was already an historic ship, having pioneered Pacific whaling in 1818. In December 1822, the same year that Captain Absalom Boston had mastered the *Industry*, the *Globe* was fitted out and ready to leave harbor. The captain was twenty-one-year-old Thomas Worth.

Among the crew was a handsome, twenty-year-old harpooner named Samuel Comstock, a man who had planned a crime so heinous his name would forever be synonymous with murder and barbarous mutiny.

At the age of thirteen Comstock ran away from his strict Quaker father and went to sea. By the time he was nineteen he had made two whaling voyages to the Pacific and advanced to a harpooner. Comstock grew to become a cruel bully whose solution to problems usually involved violence. On one of his voyages Comstock had been smitten by the beauty and tranquillity of the Pacific Islands. Unlike a lot of seamen who deserted and became beachcombers, Comstock was driven by his belief that he was not like other men and needed to have a kingdom of his own. He could think of nothing else and carefully made plans to that end. He was quite mad, but his madness made him patient and cunning.

Once at sea, Captain Worth befriended Comstock, overlooking the signs of his mental deterioration. Comstock was brutal to the men and used every opportunity to turn the men against the captain and officers. For some reason — sabotage perhaps — the food spoiled. This gave Comstock the opportunity to further undermine Worth's authority.

At the close of 1823, the *Globe* reached Hawaii. Comstock had been bullying the men so hard, six crew members deserted. This was all part of a carefully laid out plan. Captain Worth signed on six new hands, with Comstock's recommendation, among them a steward, William Humphries, an African American.

The six new recruits were riffraff, shiftless, and loyal to no one, but they were exactly what Comstock needed. On the night of January 26, 1824, Comstock, along with Silas Payne, John Oliver, and William Humphries, brutally murdered the captain and three mates with an ax, and threw them overboard. Comstock had all the weapons so the rest of the crew couldn't stop him.

Crazed and dripping in the blood of innocent men, Comstock declared himself captain of the ship and ordered the crew to throw off everything that had anything to do with whaling except the whaleboats. Then he set off to an island where he planned to kill all the crew and use the ship's timbers to build himself a castle.

Comstock's madness became more and more obvious as the days progressed. Some of his cohorts, Humphries in particular, must have had second thoughts. Humphries found a loaded pistol, but Comstock found out about it and put the steward on trial before a jury of four men, who had no choice but to find him guilty of plotting against "the captain" — Comstock.

Sentenced to death by hanging, Humphries was

given "fourteen seconds to have his say." He replied, "When I was born, little did I know I should ever come to this . . ." And at that point, Comstock ordered the bell to be rung. Then Humphries was hanged by all hands pulling him aloft. In Comstock's mind, it was fair because no one person was responsible.

At last the ship came to the Marshall Islands, where Comstock had selected Mili as his paradise home. The inhabitants seemed friendly enough, so he told William Lay and Cyrus Hussey, two young men who were not part of the mutiny, to help him move provisions off the ship. While they were on the island, the comutineers became suspicious of Payne's intentions to kill them, so they killed Comstock instead.

Meanwhile, Gilbert Smith, a member of the original crew, recruited several of the men to join him in a getaway plan. Using the confusion on the island as the opportunity and under the cover of darkness, they sailed away on the *Globe.*

On July 7, 1824, the *Globe* arrived in Valparaiso, Chile, and before the end of November the remaining crew was back in Nantucket to tell one of the goriest stories ever told.

In August 1825, the United States schooner *Dolphine* set out from Peru to find the *Globe*'s lost mutineers on Mili. When the ship arrived, two pathetic young men, burned brown by the sun, identified them-selves as Lay and Hussey, the two men who had been left behind. They had been living among the people of several small islands after Payne and the others had been killed by the inhabitants of Mili island. It seems the mutineers had mistreated the villagers and they had stoned them to death. Lay and Hussey were saved by two couples who adopted them into their families.

Herman Melville noted in his novel *Omoo* that beachcombers had a terrible reputation. And stories like the *Globe* incident didn't help change attitudes about them. "They are, mostly, a reckless, rollicking set," Melville wrote, "wedded to the Pacific, and never dreaming of ever doubling Cape Horn again on a homeward-bound passage. Hence their reputation is a bad one."

There were over 150 whale-ship deserters living in Hawaii in 1825 — a large number of them African Americans. Much to the chagrin of some American whites, blacks, both free and runaways, were accepted among the islanders with no reservations regarding skin color. But the deserters and beachcombers were not as bad as some accounts have made them out to be. According to the author George Francis, in many cases black and white seamen "played an important role as cultural middlemen, teaching useful skills with the new metal tools, acting as interpreters and business agents ...”

Many blacks had very little to return to and simply spent their entire lives moving from one port to the next to the next. For white seamen the longing for home was stronger. When they tired of lounging around doing nothing, many of them signed up on a returning whaler — preferably a “hen ship,” one in which the captain brought along his wife.

SEAFARING WOMEN

There is a story that a Nantucket whaleman was out to sea when he realized that he hadn't said good-bye to his wife. After thinking about it, he decided that it wasn't so bad, he would be away *only two years.*

Whaling voyages were long and dangerous, but the women left behind faced hard times as well. Houses built near the sea had “widow's walks,” platforms on top of houses where women gathered to look out at the sea, searching the horizon for signs of ships — hopefully their husbands' ships.

While the men were away, their daughters grew up and developed into young women. Sons had become men, many with families of their own. Returning seamen found members of their family had died, married, finished school, started a business, and even gone off to sea themselves.

Mary Hayden Russell, the wife of Captain Laban Russell, was a whaleman's wife who knew the hardships of being away from her husband years at a time. As was the custom, she met her husband and son, who was a boat steerer, in London during a shore leave. When her husband's ship departed in 1822, she remained on board with him, and thus Mary Russell became the first of a number of New England whaling wives.

In 1858, according to the Reverend Samuel Damon of Honolulu, "A few years ago it was exceedingly rare for a whaling captain to be accompanied by his wife and children, but it is now very common. An examination of the list of whalers shows that no less than 42 are now in the Pacific. Just one half of that number are now in Honolulu. This happy influence of this goodly number of ladies is apparent to the most careful observer."

Known as the captain's "best mate," a whaling wife was often the one who nursed the sick, planned healthy menus and insisted upon better prepared food, taught the seamen how to read and write, and in general soothed much of the harshness associated with whaling voyages.

Mary Chipman Lawrence was a whaling wife on the *Addison* with her husband Samuel. It is from her journal that we learn a great deal about life on board a whaler for women and children. Mary's first voyage began in November, 1856, when she sailed with her husband and five-year-old daughter, Minnie. A journal entry dated December 25 described how Christmas was celebrated:

> *"When I left port I congratulated myself that I had been in Honoluly for seven weeks and escaped the "boohoo" or "Maui" fever, to which all foreigners are subject. But my congratulations came too soon, for after being at sea several days, the boohoo seized me, and I was sick enough; obliged to keep my bed for a week. . . . Minnie hung up her stocking as usual last night and was fortunate in finding it quite well filled with the usual supply of candies, nuts, and oranges, also a book and transparent slate from me, and a $2.50 gold piece from her papa. A few days ago Mr. Forsyth, our mate, gave her a very pretty little spyglass, which she said she should call her Christmas present too."*

Sailors generally liked a ship with the captain's wife on board but sometimes she could cause problems.

One wife wrote that the first mate was "without exception, nearest to a savage of anyone I ever met." On the other hand, the mate wrote of the captain's wife, "She is the meanest, most hoggish and greediest female that ever existed. Her looks are despised by everyone on board . . ."

Among the African-American seafaring women during the Age of Sail, Nancy Gardner Prince is one of the most memorable. She was born into a whaling family in 1799 in Newburyport, Massachusetts. Her father, Thomas Gardner, was a Nantucket whaleman and when he died, Nancy's mother married an African who had escaped from a slave ship and become a sailor.

When Nancy was fifteen she moved to Boston. At twenty-five she married Nero Prince, who had been a sailor and had sailed to St. Petersburg, Russia, on a merchant ship. There he found work in the palace of the czar. The whaling industry needed huge amounts of sails and rope. A large quantity of raw materials to make them were imported from Russia.

Nancy wrote in her diary that in Russia "the color of one's skin does not prohibit one from any place or station that he or she may be capable of occupying."

The cold Russian winters took a toll on Nero, so they reluctantly decided to return to the United States. Leaving ahead of Nero, Nancy returned to Boston in

1833. Before the couple could reunite, Nero died in Russia.

Nancy's life experiences made her an advocate of freedom and justice and she devoted her life to ending slavery as an active member of the Massachusetts Anti-Slavery Society and as a teacher. One story she told was about how she had boldly helped defend a runaway from a slave catcher. As part of her work, Nancy also made many voyages to the Caribbean, especially Jamaica, where she taught school.

SISTER SAILOR

There are many unusual stories about ships and sailors, but none more interesting than this one. Newspapers in 1852 reported the following incident, which involved a "certain crew member of the *Mitchell*." The story was also reported in the journal of Nelson Cole Haley, harpooner on the *Charles W. Morgan*, as he had heard it from the captain of the *Mitchell*.

Among the greenhorns who sailed from Nantucket in 1851 was a young man who though small proved himself quite capable. "After recovering from a severe attack of seasickness, he came on deck and soon was amongst the foremost attending to the duties of the ship, being about the first to steer a good trick at the wheel, and go aloft to loose or furl and royal," reported the captain. And when they hunted the whale the captain said, "He pulled his oar with the stoutest, showing no more fear of a whale than the bravest of the green hands," and in all things he won the respect of his fellow shipmates and the goodwill of the captain and officers. He was shy and didn't talk much, but the men allowed that he was from a well-to-do family, given he didn't swear and spoke the language well.

One night, the young man became ill, hot with fever. The guard standing the graveyard watch went down into the forecastle to light his cigar. Suddenly he came running back. "Sir," he said, sputtering to one of the mates, "that young fellow who is sick is a woman. He is a she!"

They went down into the crew quarters, and sure enough, there was a young woman who, in her feverish state, had pushed the covers back exposing her upper body. The officer covered her immediately and summoned the captain, who moved her to his quarters. There she was nursed back to health. When the fever broke, she finally told the captain what had happened. In telling the story, the captain withheld her real name, so it is not known.

The sister seaman had come from a small town on the Hudson River. She fell in love with a rascal, and her well-to-do family objected to their marriage. He lured the young woman to New York City where after a few weeks he deserted her. She then hired a detective and traced her lover's whereabouts to a shipping office from where he reportedly had gone to sea on a whaler.

Determined to find him, the woman decided to follow him. She disguised herself as a boy and signed on a whaler, too. After a few weeks, she was on Nantucket and shipping out. The rest of her story they all knew.

The captain sailed to Lima, Peru, where he contacted the American consul and her passage home was arranged. On the day the sister sailor left the ship, dressed in borrowed clothing from the men, she shook each man's hand. To the mate who had discovered her she was heard to whisper, "The officers of this ship are gentlemen, and have my heartfelt thanks, but you in your kind actions on the night of my discovery, I shall remember as long as I am alive."

The woman's name was not used in either source, presumably to protect her from unwanted publicity. Although there were many seafaring women — some even served as pilots, cooks, and navigators — few if any women served as *crew members* on a whaler.

CHAPTER EIGHT

JOURNEY'S END

WHALEMEN AND THE CIVIL WAR

Abraham Lincoln, a Republican from Illinois, was elected president of the United States in November, 1860. By Christmas of that year, South Carolina had seceded from the Union. The Civil War began in April, 1861, when shots were fired on Fort Sumter, off the coast of Charleston, South Carolina. Battles were fought on land and sea and many of them involved whalers and whalemen. The first whaler to be sunk was the *Atlantic*, blasted by a Confederate privateer just a few weeks after the war began.

In October, 1861, government agents came up with a plan to block Charleston and Savannah harbors by sinking whale ships in both harbors. The Yankee whalers threw themselves into the venture wholeheartedly. The ships were purchased, then loaded with stones brought in from farmers' fields from all corners of New England.

"The Stone Fleet" set sail from New Bedford, heading south, amid cheers and gun salutes. Fifteen ships were sunk in the harbor at Charleston on December 20, 1861, and twenty-odd more a month later. The blockade attempt failed, however, because the waters were too deep.

Meanwhile, there were plenty of good ships at sea hunting whales, and their cargo was valuable and a critical part of New England's economy. Defenseless and slow, whalers became targets for Confederate warships.

The Confederate steamer *Alabama*, commanded by Captain Raphael Semmes, a Marylander, was sent on a mission to hunt down whalers. The first to be attacked was the *Ocmulgee*, whose captain was Abraham Osborne, from Edgartown, Martha's Vineyard.

The *Ocmulgee* was hunting near the Azores, and the crew was cutting in or processing a whale. Suddenly, the *Alabama* came upon them. Given the communications of that day, the whalemen might not have even known their country was in a civil war. Captain Osborne was brought to the *Alabama*, where he was taken before Captain Semmes. Osborne recognized Semmes because he had once visited his home on

Martha's Vineyard and eaten at his table. Osborne reminded Semmes of their meeting, but Semmes was not moved. The rebel captain ordered that the whaler's crew be taken off the ship and put ashore on an island in the Azores. Then the *Ocmulgee* and its whale oil was set afire.

The *Alabama* was responsible for destroying at least seventy Union vessels, among them fourteen whalers. The *Alabama* was captured and destroyed off the coast of France by the U.S.S. *Kearsarge*. Few people know about these Civil War actions.

In one of the most daring military actions of the war, Robert Smalls, a slave and pilot, sailed the *Planter*, a steamer, out of Charleston Harbor on May 13, 1862, and presented it to the U.S. Navy. After the war, Smalls served as a United States congressman.

Even when the war had officially ended in April 1865, the cruiser *Shenandoah*, commanded by Captain James Waddell, sailed around Cape Horn to the Bering Straits, where whalers were preoccupied with June bowhead whale hunting. Loaded with oil, the ships were caught off guard when the *Shenandoah* appeared out of the fog like a phantom. Without arms and slow in the water, the whale ships were like sitting ducks ready to explode into flames. Thirty-four whale ships were burned and destroyed easily. Though the war had ended the *Shenandoah* continued to destroy Yankee whalers. Some historians believe Waddell knew the war was over, but vengefully destroyed the ships.

After the Civil War, the New England whaling fleet was severely damaged. But whaling had been declining anyway since oil was discovered in Titusville, Pennsylvania, by Edwin L. Drake in 1859. And the whale population had been severely decreased. Arctic waters were by then the last profitable whaling zone, so it was more convenient to outfit and leave from west coast harbors such as San Francisco.

Now the crews of whaling ships also dramatically changed. Whaling was as dirty and dangerous as ever and the pay was still very poor, so young white men were attracted to the better-paying mill and factory jobs. But newly freed slaves, who were accustomed to hard work for no pay, jumped at the opportunity to join a whaling crew, because it allowed them to travel freely and earn wages even though they were very low. By the late 1870s, over half of the whaling crews were black; some had an even higher percentage.

One of the most well-known whalemen of color during the latter half of the nineteenth century was Captain William T. Shorey.

Born in Barbados, William T. Shorey was drawn to the whaling industry, because he was accepted on the basis of skill rather than color. Like most young men of his day, Shorey was anxious for a chance to see the world and to find his place in it.

Leaving his homeland on a whaler as a "greenhand," he shipped out in 1876 from Provincetown, Massachusetts, for his first Arctic whaling mission. In 1871 the Arctic whaling fleet had been caught by an early winter and their ships were frozen or crushed by the ice floes. Over 1,206 men and women took to the open sea in boats. They had rowed for eighty miles through Arctic gales to meet seven vessels that had escaped. Not one person was killed. However, sixty-eight whale ships were destroyed.

Shorey returned to sea as a boat steerer (or harpooner) and by 1880 he had moved through the ranks and become an officer. Sailing from Boston on November 8, 1880, as third mate of the *Emma F. Herriman*, he spent the next three years hunting whales in the Pacific and the Arctic. Reaching the rank of captain in 1886, Shorey became the only black captain in the New Bedford fleet. To be closer to the bowhead whaling grounds in the Bering Straits, whale ships began leaving San Francisco instead of New Bedford, and the Shoreys moved there in 1886.

Julia Shorey was a whaling wife who accompanied her husband on several voyages to the Pacific and the Sea of Japan. But when their two daughters, Zenobia and Victoria, were born, Julia chose to stay in San Francisco. Occasionally the family would visit their father in foreign ports.

Meanwhile, Captain Shorey mastered fourteen voyages over the next twenty-two years. Shorey's final command was on board the *John and Winthrop*. He made five voyages in this bark between 1903 and 1908. But the whaling industry was dead and dying. Pressed by the competition of electricity and crude oil, the price of whalebone and oil steadily declined so that it was no longer profitable to outfit a whaler. Shorey retired in 1908 and died a decade later in Oakland, California. His was one of the last whaling families.

Although whaling would last for several more decades, it was neither necessary nor profitable. As if to punctuate the end of an era, the *Viola*, the last wooden whaling ship built in America, departed from New Bedford on September 5, 1917. It was never heard from again.

*   *   *

A brave sight it was to see some approaching vessel fold her wings one after another as she neared the land, curtsying as she trod down the long swells; to watch her draw nearer; the bubbles breaking in a myriad of fairy bells beneath her sharp forefoot, the long swish of water murmuring against her sides; to hear the clatter of the blocks and the calling out of the men while she swept slowly past; and finally to hear the hoarse roar of the cable as she rounded to and came to rest. Squaring her yards and rising to the swell with queenly grace.

This Was the Way It Was
REX CLEMENTS

A P P E N D I X

THE WHALES THEY HUNTED

Around 1700, a whale was killed off the shore of Nantucket. The whale was much larger than the right whale, and when it was tried out, it made more and better oil than any other catch the whalemen knew. It was a spermaceti whale, also called a sperm whale. Peleg Folger, a well-known whaleman, wrote that "it has no bone in his head and his brains is all oyl." Unlike the right whale, which had two spout holes, the sperm whale had only one. And the main difference in the sperm whale was that it had teeth and it was a fighter.

Most men thought of the whale as a big fish. They did not think of it as a mammal living in the water. To them they were "fishing." But there were men who were interested in what they were hunting and tried to study the whale. Dean C. Wright was a boat steerer on a forty-six-month whaling voyage between 1841 and 1845. He wrote *Commonplace Book*, which contains, in a refreshing way, a firsthand look at whale hunting. Wright's knowledge was limited by the biological information that was available at that time.

All whales are cetaceans, derived from the Latin word *cetus*, which means "whale." Included among the seventy-seven species of cetaceans are porpoises and dolphins. There are two types of whales — the toothed whales and the baleen whales. The toothed whales have teeth. Baleen are strips of hard, bony fiber that hang from the roof of the mouth of the whale and act as a sieve. They allow the water to drain out, leaving small fish and other sea creatures behind for the whale to eat. Baleen whales have two external blowholes, while toothed whales have one.

THE BALEEN WHALES

The Blue Whale is the largest creature living on earth, stretching out to 110 feet long and weighing 130 to 150 tons.

The Fin Whale is the second largest whale, measuring eighty feet long and weighing eighty to one hundred tons. It can be distinguished from the "Big Blue" by its dark gray coloring, white lower jaw, and dorsal fin. It is

WHALE SHAPES AND SIZES COMPARED   Larry Foster

bowhead whale
Balaena mysticetus

pygmy right whale
Caperea marginata

right whale
Eubalaena glacialis

blue whale
Balaenoptera musculus

minke whale
Balaenoptera acutorostrata

fin whale
Balaenoptera physalus

humpback whale
Megaptera novaeangliae

gray whale
Eschrichtius robustus

killer whale
Orcinus orca

susu
Platanista gangetica

Amazon River dolphin
Inia geoffrensis

narwhal
Monodon monoceros

pilot whale
Globicephala melaena

sperm whale
Physeter catodon

pygmy sperm whale
Kogia breviceps

humans
Homo sapiens

harbor porpoise
Phocoena phocoena

dense-beaked whale
Mesoplodon densirostris

common dolphin
Delphinus delphis

strap-toothed whale
Mesoplodon layardi

bottlenosed dolphin
Tursiops truncatus

African elephant
Loxodonta africana

giant bottlenose whale
Berardius bairdi

Brachiosaurus
the largest dinosaur

Cuvier's beaked whale
Ziphius cavirostris

LF

METERS   5   10   15   20   25   30

[The Kendall Whaling Museum]

134

called the "greyhound of the sea" because it can travel thirty miles an hour.

The Right Whale is black in color and very slow-moving. It has an abundance of oil and baleen that grows on plates that are about seven feet across. The whale can grow as long as sixty feet and up to sixty tons.

The Bowhead Whale has the longest baleen, fourteen feet and longer in length. It is primarily black in color and can be readily identified by its bowed head. It is usually sixty-five feet long and weighs up to sixty-five tons or more. It is hunted mostly by native Alaskans.

The Humpback Whale has long flippers that make it appear that the whale has wings. It is black and gray, and gray and white. It grows up to fifty feet and reaches weights of forty-five tons.

The Gray Whale was hunted to the brink of extinction twice, in the 1600s and in the 1850s. It weighs up to thirty-seven tons, and is the size of five African elephants.

The Minke Whale is usually only thirty feet long and weighs seven to ten tons. It was named after a

Norwegian whaler, Meineke, who took this smallest of the baleen whales for the mighty Big Blue. His fellow whalers poked fun at him by calling the whale the Minke whale. They are black and gray with white bellies.

THE TOOTHED WHALES

The Sperm Whale has the largest brain, weighing twenty pounds or more. It is also the largest predator. It is probably the most recognized because it is drawn the most. It grows up to fifty feet and weighs up to sixty tons. It is dark gray or brown, and eats giant squid that weigh 4,500 pounds. Inside the huge head, which makes up one-third of its body, is a large quantity of oil. The teeth were used by carvers. It can dive up to 6,500 feet and stay under water for up to two hours. Ambergris, a product found in the intestinal bile of the whale, was used to make perfume.

The Orca (Killer) Whale grows to thirty feet and weighs eight tons or less. It has six-foot dorsal fins, and ten to thirteen conical teeth on each jaw. It eats squid, birds, seals, turtles, porpoises, and whales. It is believed that the orca was originally known as "the whale killer" and therefore became known as the "killer" whale. This suggests that it is like the shark, but the orca does not attack.

The Pilot Whale grows to twenty feet, and has a large, bulbous forehead. It has a stocky, elongated body and prominent dorsal fins and is slate gray to black in color. It travels in herds of up to one hundred, and often in the company of bottle-nosed dolphins.

The Narwhal Whale is recognizable by its tooth, which grows through the upper lip into an eight-foot tusk. It appears to be a spear. Native Alaskans prize the Narwhal's tusk. The whale is stocky and slow, with dark blue or gray spots on its white skin. It can grow to be fifteen feet long and weigh 3,500 pounds.

The Beluga Whale is white. It is sometimes called the "sea canary" because of its vocalizations. It squeals, chirps, and clicks in ranges that contain more variation than most other whales. It has a small head. The whale grows up to sixteen feet and weighs up to 2,400 pounds. It lives in the Arctic waters.

Bottle-nosed dolphins, common dolphins, white-sided dolphins, and harbor porpoises are part of the whale family as well.

IMPORTANT DATES

1441 The Portuguese government claims the Cape Verde Islands off the coast of West Africa. Africans on both sides of the continent hunt whales by leaping on the whale's back and clogging its blowholes.

1565 A Basque whaling ship, the *San Juan,* sinks off the coast of Labrador. European presence in the Americas as whalers is well established.

1602 Captain Bartholomew Gosnold explores Cape Cod, Nantucket, Martha's Vineyard, and the Cuttyhunk Islands and claims them for the British.

1619 Twenty African captives are brought to Virginia as indentured servants.

1638 Slave uprising in colonial Boston.

1641 Massachusetts is first colony to legalize chattel slavery;

New York and New Jersey institute slavery in 1664 and Connecticut follows in 1650.

1647 George Fox organizes the Society of Friends, also known as the Quakers, in England. They are persecuted for their beliefs.

1650 Shore whaling is a prosperous business for Long Islanders.

1712 Slave revolt in New York. Captain Christopher Hussey captures a sperm whale out at sea. Nantucket becomes center of whaling.

1716 Slaves brought to Nantucket Island. They help build the shore-whaling business.

1770 Seaman Crispus Attucks dies in the Boston Massacre. Slavery abolished on the island of Nantucket.

1773 Two whalers, the *Dartmouth* and the *Beaver*, are involved in the Boston Tea Party.

1775 First abolitionist society in United States is started in Philadelphia on April 14.

1776 Declaration of Independence signed. Revolutionary War devastates the whaling industry.

1777 Vermont becomes first state to legally abolish slavery.

1783 Slavery is abolished in Massachusetts.

1787 U. S. Constitution approved with clauses that protect slavery and slaveholders.

1800 Gabriel Prosser's revolt in Richmond, Virginia.

1805 Famous African-American shipbuilder, John Mashow born in Massachusetts.

1810 Underground Railroad escape routes involve uses of the sailor's protection certificates.

1816 African Methodist Episcopal Church is officially organized. Captain Paul Cuffe transports thirty-eight blacks on his ship and at his own expense to Sierra Leone as part of a Back-to-Africa movement. Many blacks opposed his movement.

1819 The *Essex* leaves on its ill-fated voyage. The following year it is rammed by a raging bull sperm whale. Survivors are forced into cannibalism.

1820 *Mayflower of Liberia* transports sixty-eight free blacks to Monrovia as a mutual effort by some whites and blacks to return freed slaves to Africa.

1822 Former seaman Denmark Vesey, organizes a slave uprising in Charleston, South Carolina, but he is betrayed by an informer. Captain Absalom Boston departs Nantucket on a whaling voyage with an all-black crew.

Mary Russell becomes first captain's wife to travel on a whaling voyage.

1823 Whites and black residents help a fugitive slave family hide from slave catchers on the island of Nantucket.

1824 Mutiny on the *Globe.*

1831 William Lloyd Garrison publishes first issue of *The Liberator*, an abolitionist newspaper.

1834 Slavery ends in British empire.

1838 Frederick Douglass escapes to freedom by using a borrowed Sailor's Protection Certificate.

1841 Frederick Douglass makes his first abolitionist speech on Nantucket Island, on August 11. The United States Supreme Court frees Cinque and the other *Amistad* rebels; they are allowed to return to Africa. There is a slave revolt on the *Creole*, which was bound for New Orleans from Hampton, Virginia. Rebels take over the ship and sail it to the Bahamas where they are greeted as heroes.

1842 Douglass returns to Nantucket to speak against slavery again. Some of the abolitionists harshly criticized proslavery clergy. A protest occurs in defense of the clergy that errupts into a riot.

1846 Fire devastates Nantucket's town and harbor.

1847 Frederick Douglass begins publishing *North Star*.

1849 Gold is discovered in California. Whaling crews jump ship to search for gold. Harriet Tubman escapes from slavery.

1850 There are 3.2 million slaves living in the United States. Congress passes strict Fugitive Slave Act, which makes it a federal offense to help a runaway slave.

1857 The Dred Scott decision by the United States Supreme Court denies citizenship to all blacks — whether they are slaves or free. Therefore, free blacks can't vote, hold public office, serve on juries, apply for a patent, or qualify for Sailor's Protection Certificates.

1859 Oil is discovered in Titusville, Pennsylvania.

1860 Abraham Lincoln is elected President of the United States. South Carolina secedes from the Union on December 18.

1861–65 The Civil War begins at Fort Sumter in Charleston Harbor, on April 12. In 1862, whale ships are sunk in the harbor in an attempt to blockade Charleston. The channel is too deep and the plan fails. The *Alabama*, commanded by Raphael Semmes sinks over seventy vessels, including fourteen whalers. The *Shenandoah* sinks whalers in the Arctic Ocean even after the Civil War has ended in 1865.

1865 On January 31 Congress passes the Thirteenth Amendment to the Constitution, which on ratification abolishes slavery in the United States. Slavery remains legal in Cuba and parts of South America.

1876 United States celebrates its centennial anniversary. Statue of Liberty is presented to the United States by France. William T. Shorey begins his career as a "greenie" on an Arctic whaler.

1886 Shorey becomes captain of his own whaler.

1908 Shorey retires.

1917 The *Viola*, the last wooden ship built in America, departs from New Bedford, on Saturday, September 5 (the height of hurricane season). It is never heard from again.

BIBLIOGRAPHY

Atheker, Herbert. *A History of the Negro People.* New York: First Carol Publishing, 1990.

Baldwin, Robert. *New England Whaler.* Minneapolis, Minnesota: Lerner Publications, 1996.

Baley, Thomas. *Sailing Ships.* New York: Sadie Fields Publication, 1997.

Bennett, Lerone. *Before the Mayflower: A History of Black America.* Second ed. Chicago: Johnson Publishing Company, 1987.

Bolster, Jeffrey. *Black Jacks: African-American Seamen in the Age of Sail.* London, England: Harvard University Press, 1997.

Carrol, Rebecca. *Sugar in Rain.* New York: Crown Trade Paperbacks, 1997.

Corrigan, Patricia. *The Whale Watchers Guide.* Wisconsin: Northward Press, 1989.

Cousteau, Jacques. *Atlas of the Oceans.* England: Reed International, 1996.

Francis, Daniel. *A History of World Whaling.* Canada: Viking, 1990.

Francis, George. *Whale Ships and Whaling.* New York: Dover Publications, 1985.

Garner, Straton. *The Captain's Best Mate.* Massachusetts: Brown University, 1966.

Hale, Thomas. *Spun Years and Scuttlebutt.* Massachusetts: Crow Nest Press, 1996.

Hannon, Frantz. *Black Skin, White Mask.* New York: Weidenfeld, 1967.

Hughill, Stan. *Shanties from the Seven Seas.* Mystic, Connecticut: Mystic Seaport Museum, 1994.

Kaplan, Sidney. *The Black Presence in the Era of the American Revolution.* Massachusetts: University of Massachusetts, 1989.

Man, John. *The History of Slavery.* New York: Chartwell Books, 1991.

Melville, Herman. *Moby Dick.* Los Angeles: The Arion Press, 1979.

Murphy, Jim. *Gone A-Whaling — The Lure of the Sea and the Hunt for the Great Whale.* New York: Clarion Books, 1998.

Paienwonsky, Isidor. *The Burning of a Pirate Ship.* New York: Fordam Press, 1992.

Tibbles, Anthony. *Transatlantic Slavery.* London, England: National Museums and Galleries, 1994.

Wilbur, Keith. *Pirates and Patriots of the Revolution.* Connecticut: The Globe Pequot Press, 1984.

Wilbur, Keith. *The New England Indians.* Connecticut: The Globe Pequot Press, 1978.

JOURNALS/PAMPHLETS

"African Americans on Martha's Vineyard." Articles from the archives of The Dukes County Historical Society, edited by Arthur Railton. Unpublished.

Floria Barnett Cash. "African American Whalers: Images and Reality." *Long Island Historical Journal.* Vol 2, No. 1, pp. 41–52 (date unknown).

William S. McFeely. "Abolitionism on Nantucket: Is This Not a Man?" *New England Monthly*, October 1989.

Mary Miles. "Frederick Douglass in Nantucket: An Interview with Robert F. Mooney." *Yesterday's Island/Today's Nantucket*, Vol. 21, No. 10. July (date unknown).

"Heroes in the Ships: African Americans in the Whaling Industry," a permanent exhibition of the Kendall Whaling Museum, Sharon, Massachusetts, 1990.

The Duke County Intelligencer. Duke County Historical Society. Massachusetts: August 1964 Vol. 6, No. 1.

The Duke County Intelligencer. Duke County Historical Society. Massachusetts: February 1977 Vol. 4.

"Landmark in Nantucket Black History Restored." *New York Times*, January 12, 1997.

VIDEO

Moby Dick. United Artists, California, 1956.

The Whalers. Arts and Entertainment. New York, 1996.

I N D E X

151